Liquid Leadership

Liquid Leadership

Damian Hughes

CAPSTONE

978-1-90646543-8

A catalogue record for this book is available from the British Library.

Typeset in 9/10.5pt, Baskerville by Thomson Digital
Printed in the UK by TJ Interntaional, Padstow, Cornwall

Contents

Contents

Acknowledgements

I would like to thank the following people for their invaluable and incredible help and support during the process of writing this book.

Geraldine – Thank you for your incredible support, belief, encouragement, insights, patience and skill. Thanks for continuing to inspire and amaze me. This book belongs to you.

Mum and Dad – Thank you for your continued help, advice, encouragement, support and inspiration.

Chris and Jody Hughes – the greatest mates anyone could ask for. Thanks for your support.

Joseph Hughes – a future legend. Welcome to the gang!

Anthony Hughes – Thanks for your continued encouragement and backing. It means a great deal.

Mari Griffin – Thank you for bringing your own unique brand of magic to bear and making the book readable!

Gerry Griffin – thanks for your fantastic help and support.

Stephen, Sue, Max, Jake, Ben Griffin – Thanks for the help, advice, support and laughs.

Chris Mallaband – the original "liver of a life less ordinary". Thanks for your continued advice and backing.

David Manson – Thanks for your genuine help and support and astute advice and counsel. It has been a great help.

Andrew Park, www.cognitivemedia.com – Thank you for your continued support, belief and backing. It is incredible.

Chris Bond and SBCA Accountancy – Many thanks for being a great source of help, support and advice. A true accounting wizard.

Bill Sweetenham – Thank you for your support and advice.

Sir Alex Ferguson – Thank you for sharing some of your wisdom. It is much appreciated.

James Timpson – Thanks for your time, humour and candour. It was invaluable.

Fergus Finlay – I am grateful for your openness and genuine support, which has been incredible.

Kim England – Thanks for your courage and candour. A future spent inspiring others now beckons.

Kevin Sinfield – Thank you for your openness, trust and help. Keep on leading and inspiring others.

Simon Clifford – the first of what will be many books about you. Thanks for your trust, humour and support.

Phil Ince – a great source of help, advice and – above all – friendship. Thanks, mate.

Martin Perry – Thank you for your challenges and wise counsel.

Tony Smith – Thank you for your trust and candour.

Emma Finlay – Thanks for your advice, knowledge and support. I look forward to reading your own story soon.

All Liquid Thinkers and Liquid Leaders everywhere – Thanks for the inspiration!

Forza Malaka!

About the author

Damian Hughes is the founder of the LiquidThinker Company, which takes the methods used by great achievers and shows, in easy steps, how you can adopt them into your own life and business in order to achieve your dreams and ambitions. He is the author of *Liquid Thinking* and *The Survival Guide to Change*.

Hughes, a former England schoolboy footballer and Manchester United football coach, was a human resources director for Unilever and led a turnaround in performance at the UK's oldest manufacturing site in Port Sunlight before carrying out similar work in Africa and the US.

He now runs his own change management consultancy, LiquidThinker Ltd, helping a wide range of individuals, teams and industries achieve similar employee engagement and success. He also works as sports psychologist for the GB Rugby League team.

Hughes runs a Manchester inner-city youth club, Collyhurst and Moston, which has helped reduce crime and helped many kids find a purpose in their lives, from stopping crime to winning Olympic medals. He was also nominated for the 2007 William Hill Sports book of the year award for his biography of boxing great Sugar Ray Robinson.

His innovative and exciting approach has been praised by Sir Richard Branson, Muhammad Ali, Sir Terry Leahy, Tiger Woods, Jonny Wilkinson and Sir Alex Ferguson.

If you are interested in Damian working with you, contact him at damian@liquidthinker.com or visit his website at www.liquidthinker.com.

Foreword

My Manchester United players have established a reputation for being tough but also for playing fair, which is a discipline that I have worked hard to instil in them as I believe that it is a fundamental requirement to get through life.

Before I got to where I am today, I had to have a beginning and I believe that I had a great upbringing to prepare me for my later years. I have many recollections which I fall back on from my childhood and a lot of them helped to create the foundation of my character and personality as a leader.

Everybody played football and it was always a competitive environment, but this healthy competition created a will to win that encourages real leadership qualities to emerge. This taught me discipline and a loyalty to friends and it was also responsible for the drive and perseverance which you need to be successful, and these traits have never left me, simply because I could not let down those who helped me all those years ago. They invested their time in me, and I believe in fulfilling that sacrifice.

I hope that these reflections help and encourage you to read this book, because Damian has captured many of the important points about what a leader needs to do. The important things to succeed are a real work ethos, discipline, determination and a respect for others.

Good luck.

Sir Alex Ferguson CBE
Manager, Manchester United Football Club

Preface

Bill Sweetenham was the National Performance Director for Great Britain's swimming team from 2000 to 2007. He managed the Australian swimming team for four Olympic Games and five Commonwealth Games. He was also the head of the Australian Institute of Swimming from the late 1980s until 1994, and was the National Youth Coach for Swimming Australia. He has worked with more than 12 world record holders as part of the national team in Australia. He was voted Australian coach of the year three times, and as National Performance Director in Britain he led the national team to 15 medals at the 2001 and 2003 world championships.

As someone who has trained over 12 world record holders, 40 Olympians and numerous world-class athletes, I have been afforded a unique insight into the mind of exceptional performers; people who have been willing to stand apart from the masses and to pursue their own dreams, regardless of what anyone else says or thinks; people who have made sacrifices to be able to live their own vision of success; and people who have displayed incredible per-sistence until they have achieved it. In short, people who have stepped up to the plate and taken the lead.

These insights have shown me that these characteristics, which all great leaders possess, can be learned but with just one rule. You must want it enough.

I would encourage you to read Damian's book with a mind that is open to challenge and open to new ideas and to think about situations in your life where you can take a lead, whatever your current status or position.

Finally, and this is the most important lesson of all, I would urge you to try them! You will surprise yourself with your true abilities.

Enjoy the book and your own leadership journey.

Bill Sweetenham

Why read this book?

> **66** *If you think that you are too small to make a difference, try going to bed with a mosquito in your room.* **99**

DAME ANITA RODDICK (1942–2007)

Anita Roddick's comment captures the whole point of this book. The book is aimed at anyone. It isn't the sole preserve of those who already hold leadership positions at work, in the community or within a family. We all have the ability to take a lead and this book is aimed at helping you recognize that, then to step forward and make a difference.

I have two requests before you read any further:

1. Make yourself vulnerable.

2. Have a pen with you when you read.

I want you to make yourself as vulnerable as possible when you pick up this book. This seems a strange request to make, so let me explain further.

On a coaching course I attended a number of years ago, the trainer wrote a message on the board that said "vulnerability = power". I didn't understand this at first. Being a competitive sort, I had always imagined that power was all about force, domination, even intimidation; in short, power was about being the fountain of all knowledge. Instead, as the trainer explained, if you change your definition of power to be about having the ability to motivate, inspire and change your life and the lives of others around you, then nothing is more powerful than being vulnerable and admitting that you don't have all the answers.

Cyclist Lance Armstrong is an example to illustrate this point. It was only when he was diagnosed with cancer and was struggling for his life that the young, rich, seemingly unbreakable athlete became vulnerable for the first time. When he finally had to admit his vulnerability, he discovered the key to unlocking his own extraordinary potential as an athlete, a person and a leader.

If you have picked up this book and are determined to read it with a cynical mind, believing that there is nothing you can learn, or determined to find fault or criticism with what is contained in the pages, then I have no doubt that you will be successful in your aim. But what then? What else will you have gained? Instead, by choosing to make yourself vulnerable, you open your mind to the possibility of learning something that will make you more powerful.

Secondly, too many books of this nature can often end up forming part of your shelf development–they end up looking good on your bookshelf rather than ever being put to any practical use. Scribble ideas in this book and underline notes, quotes or answers. This is your book, so use it to try out ideas and challenge your thinking about how to be a better leader. At the back of the book I have included some exercises relating to each chapter. When you have finished reading, have a look and try some of them out.

Finally, as singer Ian Brown from the Stone Roses suggests, "it doesn't matter where you're from, it's where you're at" that really counts and you are now at a critical point. Only 10 per cent of books ever get read beyond the first chapter. You are now at the point of putting yourself into the minority of people who ever get past the introduction. Reading further will help you become the great leader that you are capable of being.

I began my other book *Liquid Thinking* by quoting the esteemed philosopher Jerry Springer, and I have chosen another quote from him for this book because it summarizes this introduction perfectly.

" *Nobody gives you power. You just take it!* "

So what are you waiting for?

CHAPTER 1
WELL OF COURAGE

" Courage is rightly esteemed the first of human qualities, because it is the quality which guarantees all others. "

SIR WINSTON CHURCHILL (1874–1965)

Carpe Diem! Stand up and be counted! Put your neck on the block! Take the bull by the horns! Grasp the nettle . . .

When a subject is as rich in metaphors as courage, there must be lots to learn about it. Given the obvious importance of courage to successful leadership, it is amazing to note how little coverage it receives. There are loads of books about risk avoidance and management and very little about the positive nature of courage. It's like going into a bookshop to buy the *Joy of Sex* and being told that there is nothing on this subject, but over 20 different books on reducing impotence. While courage is no guarantee of success, it is obvious that taking action without displaying some sort of bravery is an effective way of preventing success.

The nineteenth-century German philosopher Arthur Schopenhauer believed that all ideas have to go through three clear stages:

1. They are ridiculed.

2. They are violently opposed.

3. They are accepted as self-evident.

Apply these three stages to Rosa Parks, the Alabama mother who refused to accept that because of the colour of her skin she should be forced to sit at the back of a public bus. She recalled, "I knew someone had to take the first step and I made up my mind not to move." Initially, her decision was ridiculed ("who was *she* to dare to ignore the rules?") before it manifested itself in violent civil rights clashes. Can you imagine now suggesting that there should be a colour bar on buses? Of course not. The courage that Rosa showed when she made her decision is now self-evident.

Courage is vital in taking that first step and so why don't we see more of it? You can find a clue in one long word: *allodoxaphobia*, the fear of being ridiculed by other people. It is one of the most common phobias in the UK and it affects everyone to some degree. This means that the easier option is often to play safe and behave in a way that means we will fit in and be fully accepted by others, so we hold back from doing and saying what we really want. Courage is vital to break through this fear.

Don't believe me? I have regularly tested this concept out with a simple experiment on a number of different groups and audiences, of all ages and ranges of experience, where I take £10 out of my pocket, hold it up and ask if anyone wants the money. You would think that would be a no-brainer, wouldn't you? Who would say no to free money? The outcome is always the same. Silence. Followed by a little more silence, followed by nervous laughter. I even hear people telling their friends to go up and get the money. Eventually someone runs up and grabs the money out of my hand, at which point everyone claps and the lucky winner immediately tries to give the money back – even though it was offered to them with no strings attached! There is one reason I am never trampled by a rush of people coming to grab the money. It is that voice in your head (if you're wondering "Which voice?", it's that one!) which is shouting, "It's an evil trick! If I run up there to collect the money everyone will laugh at me. I don't understand the game. It can't be that simple. I'll make a fool of myself."

That's allodoxaphobia in action.

What is courage? My own favourite definition of the word is the original meaning of it, which is "to speak your own mind with all your heart".

This means that courage is something that is profoundly personal and intimate to only you. Many of the people who have won the Victoria Cross (which is the highest military award for bravery issued by the British Army and has only ever been given to 1355 people in its 160-year history) have all had very different reasons for displaying courage and many of them claimed, "I only did what I had to." Courage is often something that others recognize rather than the kind of behaviour that anyone ever deliberately sets out to display.

Stop reading for a moment and consider that last sentence, because it is a crucial point.

Despite what the cowardly lion in *The Wizard of Oz* believed, courage isn't an inbuilt quality, something that you are either born with or you are not. With a bit of practice, anyone can develop the ability to be courageous. If the first step is about speaking with all your heart, it helps to know what's in your heart.

So how can you practise being courageous?

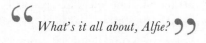

❝ *What's it all about, Alfie?* **❞**

Let's take an idea from Michael Caine that will guide you through some practical steps to improve your courage. More specifically, let's take some advice from Caine's character Alfie from the 1966 film of the same name. In this film, Alfie's monologues to the camera are inaudible to others in the scene.

Imagine that you are at work and you attend a meeting to discuss plans on how to increase morale among the workforce. You are listening to the debate when your mind suddenly recalls a crazy but intriguing idea you read about in this very book. You feel torn between saying something to the group and concern about what the response will be. It's decision time . . .

Let's now employ the technique from *Alfie* where everyone else stops and you turn to the camera to discuss the pros and cons of the action you might take. In our film there are four practical steps that you can take that will enhance your bravery. Remember, you are the director and star of this film as well, so you can choose whichever option suits you best.

Show your struggle

Let's go back to the freeze frame of the meeting at work. What are you saying to the camera?

" *Sssh. Keep quiet. Don't say a word. They'll think that I'm crazy. It's not my job to come up with ideas. Besides, it'll never work anyway. If I do say something, before this meeting is finished and they stop laughing at me the boss will have heard about it and he'll fire me. I've got a family to support. A mortgage to pay. Keep quiet.* **"**

While this might be a slight exaggeration of what you're saying, it contains some of the fears you may have, including your fear of failure, of looking stupid, of not being good enough, smart enough, clever enough or quick-witted enough. All of these fears lead to that one great fear we all dread – rejection. This means rejection from the group, including our colleagues, our friends and our family. These are the fears that play a huge role in preventing us from playing to our true potential; they strangle the new idea before it ever sees the light of day.

The entrepreneur and inventor Charles Brewer once summed up this feeling when he suggested, "A new idea is delicate. It can be killed by a yawn; it can be stabbed to death by a joke, or worried to death by a frown on the right person's brow." Somehow, a fear that goes unspoken starts to grow in the greenhouse-like atmosphere of your mind.

There is a really simple cure for fear: show that you are struggling.

Go back to that scene at work where you are struggling with what to do with the crazy idea. Instead of keeping quiet, you decide to show your colleagues that you are having some difficulties.

66 *I'm not sure how to say this . . . I'm really stuck . . . rather than bottle this up . . . can I share an idea I read recently? Is it okay to throw in an idea that I haven't really worked out yet?* 99

By not being scared of showing the pain of your struggle and indecision, you invite help. Nobody really wants to work with smart-arses who know it all. When faced with someone who is obviously stuck and is prepared to admit that they are stuck, it becomes hard not to want to help.

People who are prepared to acknowledge their own struggles like this have real courage. The possibility of being ridiculed or being on the end of a clever put-down is far outweighed by the connection and goodwill that your difficulties will generate.

The point is, when you ask for help and are not afraid to show your vulnerability, most people are psychologically conditioned to want to help you.

Be a contender

❝ *You don't understand! I could'a had class. I could'a been a contender. I could'a been somebody, instead of a bum, which is what I am.* ❞

Terry Molloy, On the Waterfront.

Let's go back to our film scene, the meeting where you kept quiet. Now let the movie run on and watch as everyone packs up their gear and starts to leave. You gather your belongings together and leave the meeting as well. You said nothing, just like everyone else. "Don't worry," that voice in your head soothes you, "it was no big deal. It doesn't matter. It wasn't even that important." But the voice won't go away. It whispers, "You had something to offer. You could have made a real difference." With regret, you start to admit to yourself that you could have said something.

Do you recognize this scene? What's happening here?

What you are actually doing is rehearsing the scene in your mind. The only problem is that the moment has passed and it's too late for a rehearsal. Rehearsals only work before the event. Few of us have the habit of rehearsing how we want things to be by running them through in our head and painting a clear picture of how things could be before they happen. Without this clear picture, it's difficult to have a belief or a conviction about what great achievements are possible; instead, fears rush in and fill the vacuum. This is how a mediocre idea is born.

One easy way you can do this is to start all of your future meetings with a couple of minutes dedicated to this mental rehearsal. You could do this privately, or you could dare to make it real and encourage others to start by thinking about the end of the day.

"Good morning everyone. Before the meeting starts, let's take a couple of minutes to imagine that it is 5.30 p.m. and we are walking out of the door. We're slapping each other on the back, feeling incredibly excited by the ideas we've had. There's a real buzz of anticipation about what's possible."

What's important here is that you are attaching yourself to a vision that is personally motivating. This picture provides you with enough motivation to step out of your comfort zone and through your fears.

You are practising the technique of visualization, which major athletes have been doing for years. It involves focusing not on the pain of speaking up but on the benefits of what you will get from actually doing it. This is the same behaviour that Tiger Woods practises every morning. Before he heads out to the golf course, he disciplines himself to visualize his best chip, his best putt and his best drive. He understands that the brain reacts to this image every bit as powerfully as if it were happening in real life, and so he prepares his brain to achieve it. If it's good enough for Tiger, why not adopt the same approach and imagine yourself in a situation where you need that extra shot of courage?

Find your friends

Unfortunately, many groups, organizations and cultures don't actively encourage or support the development of courage. Challenging the bosses isn't particularly welcomed; an off-the-wall idea is often greeted by a sarcastic quip; a brave act only offered a grudging recognition; the ideas in the suggestion box remain ignored. In such an environment, being courageous is even more difficult and many people cite this lack of support as a reason not even to bother trying.

But why do you have to embark on such a journey alone? Let's swap stories and look at J.R.R. Tolkein's classic, *The Lord of the Rings*. The little hobbit Frodo didn't set out across Middle Earth to return the ring to its home on his own. He formed a fellowship, a group where bravery could grow and flourish. Too often bravery is typecast as being a solitary activity. Take time to recognize your own Gandalf, someone to advise you when to fight and when to walk on. Who is your Aragon, your Sam or your Pippin? (You may also find one or two Gollums too). Find people who will stay by your side to share the burden and risk pulling you away from the fires of trouble.

Don't get caught up in the myth of the solitary hero. It's a lot easier to be courageous if you know that there is someone watching out for you.

Celebrate bravery

Finally, if you want people to be brave, then start recognizing them for it. Promote courage as a value of any group of which you are a part and openly start talking about those actions that fit the description. Look for signs of bravery in people who join your team. In short, encourage courage.

Southwest Airlines have a wall of fame in its headquarters that is actually a museum in honour of the company's biggest mistakes. The culture encourages bravery in employees. Herb Kelleher, the founder, argues, "We tell our people to question and challenge everything. It is decades of conventional wisdom which have sometimes led this industry into huge losses. You may make mistakes but the costs of getting burned once in a while are insignificant compared to the benefits that come from feeling free to be brave and to take risks."

Act today to create a culture that is a fertile ground for acts of courage, of bravery, of people putting their heads above the parapet, seizing the day, putting their necks on the block, standing up and being counted, taking the bull by the horns, grasping the nettle . . .

Good luck!

The risk poem

To laugh is to risk appearing a fool,

To cry is to risk appearing sentimental and soft,

To reach out to another is to risk involvement,

To show your feelings is to risk exposing your inherent self,

To place your ideas, your dreams, your desires before people is to risk their loss,

To love is to risk not being loved in return,

To show strength is to risk showing weakness,

To do is to risk failure.

The greatest hazard in life is to risk nothing,

The person who risks nothing, gets nothing, has nothing, is nothing.

He may avoid suffering, pain, sorrow, but he does not live, he does not love,

He has sold, forfeited freedom, integrity,

He is a slave, chained by safety, locked away by fear.

Because, only a person who is willing to risk not knowing the result is free.

Anonymous.

Kim England

I enjoyed a really happy and settled childhood with my mum and dad, Trisha and Richard, and my younger sister Caryn. We moved around the country as my dad's career progressed and after leaving school I moved to Cape Town to complete a three-year in-house training programme with Three Cities Hotels while completing my Psychology and Communication degree through UNISA. Having graduated, I was working as a travel consultant at two hotels while saving the money for my visa to head out to the UK with my friends.

My career up until this point had been pretty eclectic. I had worked as a travel consultant, a chef, a restaurant manager and a legal secretary, and I had experienced every role possible within the hotel industry. What I really enjoyed was the people side of my work and that is why I thrive in my current role as National Sales Training Manager for Unilever Foodsolutions in South Africa.

My life changed forever on Monday 18 January 1999.

I had worked another long day on the travel desk and had enjoyed dinner with my aunt and uncle before driving home at 11 o'clock at night. As I reversed into my parking space, I became aware of a man standing right next to my window, holding a small plastic milk bottle. It gave me a fright when I noticed him, but when I looked into his eyes, I felt a cold, paralysing fear like never before. There was nothing in his eyes, no emotion and no humanity; there was a void, an evil emptiness that I could feel through the glass. He gestured for me to open my window, which I did by a few centimetres, and he whispered, "I need your car for a robbery", at the same time revealing a large knife as a signal of his intentions.

I was terrified, and thought that there was no way I was going to stay in the car with him. I told him that he could have the car and everything in it, but he had to leave me there and he agreed. I got out of the car, clutching my handbag, which I explained held the keys to my flat and we walked very slowly, with him following only inches behind, brandishing the knife as a chilling reminder not to do anything rash. By the time we had reached the door of my flat, I had separated my car keys from my flat keys and had even given him the gate remote. In this way, I had helped him plan his escape but had also secured my safety. My only thought was that I had to live; the car was irrelevant.

I left the front door of my flat open and hoped that he would just tie me up as he had promised and then leave. Instead, he closed the door and made me lie on the floor while he tied my hands behind my back with my own belt and gagged me with a towel. When I was secured, he began to pace menacingly, asking me questions. Every couple of minutes, he would offer a grim reminder of his power by brandishing the knife and snarling, "I could kill you, you know." He asked me questions about who I lived with and

whether I had a boyfriend. I had to spit out the gag
to give him my answers.

During this period, however, the adrenalin heightened
my senses to such a degree that I was incredibly aware
of the world around me. I could hear the trees moving
outside, could feel my heart beating in my ears,
could feel his footfalls on the carpet around me and taste
the towel in my mouth and feel the thin bead of sweat that
ran down my back. After the question about my boyfriend,
he asked me whether *he* could be my boyfriend and I
chose not to respond. He suddenly knelt down in front
of my feet, pointed the knife at me and told me to take
my jeans down. Then the dark fear that I had been struggling
to keep contained suddenly became real. I was not to
escape from this ordeal by only being frightened but
possibly raped too. Still, my overriding thought was that I
wanted to live. I shook my head and he demanded I remove
my jeans.

He put on a condom, pulled down my jeans and
raped me.

He got up, took the car keys I had given him, took a last
look around, grabbed my portable stereo and walked
out, closing the door behind him. I remained on the
carpet for a beat or two, listening and visualizing him
walking down the stairs to the car park, before I got to my
feet, pulled the belt off my wrists, the towel from my
mouth, picked up my cell phone and the landline, and
simultaneously called my aunt on one and the flying
squad on the other. The time was 11.15. I had spent
15 minutes with this man and the only external

physical signs I had were a small nick on my wrist from my belt and a tiny cut on my knee, neither of which remains to this day.

Before this, I had always thought that rape was just sex and that afterwards, you would be able to rationalize it as that, a horrid physical act like badly breaking a limb, before cleaning yourself up and moving on without any real harm done to your mind. So, you can start to understand that my own reactions were not at all what was expecting. I had no idea what fear and the resulting adrenalin do to your body.

When the police arrived, I started talking and didn't stop until my statement had been taken. Although you are entitled to have access to a female officer, I just wanted to get the whole story out. I don't think they quite knew how to handle me, and if I think back now, it was the last time that I behaved like the old me before the shock kicked in and stripped all of that away. Soon, however, a sense of being numb and lethargic started to wash over me. On the way home I vomited from the horror of my ordeal. I had a bath and just sat there with no urge to scrub. I didn't feel dirty, like I had read you were supposed to. I was just numb and spaced out. I called home but I couldn't find the words to explain to my parents what had happened. I just couldn't get my tongue around it and the ability to use the word 'rape' took nearly six years to come back. It is still uncomfortable to articulate.

When I woke up a few hours later, my whole body ached with a hot heaviness that extended into my bones. I felt like an elephant was resting on my chest and my nerves were raw, ultra sensitive and exposed. It took me three days to cry and when I did, my parents recall the tears didn't run down my face but poured from my eyes. I also emitted these primal, huge noisy howls which came from the very pit of my stomach. It felt like a trap door to my soul had been opened and I couldn't stop the sounds from coming out. When I think back to this moment, it seems to me that this was the first step in my recovery as I stopped being numb and started to feel again.

Talking about it also proved a huge help. Often when there is a problem, it is easy to believe that by ignoring it, it will go away, but I was determined that there would be no hiding and pretending it had never happened. I knew that I wasn't to blame and I wasn't going to be made to feel like anything other than what I had done had been the right thing at that time.

People asked me, "Why didn't you scream, run away, drive over him, just do something?" I tell them that if they had been there, they would have known that listening to and acting on my intuition was the only thing that got me out alive. I later discovered that my attacker, who had the AIDS virus, had also been previously accused of murder, housebreaking, indecent assault, vehicle theft, the rape of others, including a minor, and operating under a number of aliases. During one escape attempt he had stabbed a policeman, severing both the arteries and veins to and from his heart and very nearly killing him. My assailant would have had no problem stabbing me if I had resisted, and I knew that when I looked at him through the car window.

Essentially, I took control of my interpretation of the event, which meant I regained a measure of control in my life. I wasn't going to let other people's interpretations affect how I dealt with the situation. If I was to heal I was going to have to seek out the assistance I needed, speak up when I felt overwhelmed and take the lead in healing the hurt that had occurred.

Fifteen minutes was the entire extent of that night's experience. I have calculated that there are nearly one million 15-minute periods in a 70-year-old person's life. There needs to be some perspective on that. Yes, those minutes were significant, but no more so than any other really powerful experience. A wedding, a birth, a swim in the sea, all can have equal weight, can change your life irrevocably, so we have just as much need to focus on those 15-minute periods that help us to grow rather than wither. I have a friend who is a mosaic artist and she describes her work as taking shattered fragments and turning them into something more beautiful than before. That is a metaphor for how I have chosen to live. I knew that I had a choice to take an event that felt like it could leave me broken and scattered, and create a new form from those pieces. Choosing to keep the good and discard the harmful is in itself a healing process.

When I look back over the last eight years of my recovery, there is one quality that I learned about myself and that I believe that everyone possesses: I have incredible reserves of stamina. I don't mean in any great or dramatic way. At first, I took my days ten seconds at a time, if that was all I could handle. I would tell myself, as I counted them down, that now I had got through those ten seconds, I could do another ten seconds, and some more and another ten seconds, until minutes and hours had gone by. I learned that the human spirit is incredibly resilient in being able to recover from almost anything. For me the reward of being whole again far outweighed the lethargy of merely existing as damaged and this spurred me on to continue looking for the healing. Living in a state of terror was totally unacceptable, unsustainable and frankly exhausting, I wasn't prepared to be that way indefinitely.

There is, however, just one piece of advice that I would like to share with you. Whatever anyone does to you physically, they cannot take away what makes you unique. You are more than your physical body – you are also a fascinating mixture of feelings, emotions, perceptions, thoughts, history and imagination. Victor Frankl wrote of his experience in the Nazi death camps that they could do what they wanted to his body, but he could decide within himself how he would let it affect him. He had the freedom to choose his response, so there was nothing that could transpire that he couldn't deal with. He moved from being a victim to having control over the emotions that occurred within him.

In my context, deciding how I interpreted those 15 minutes had a lot to do with my healing. I wasn't going to be ashamed or embarrassed. I had done what I did in order to survive, with no regrets, no looking back to say "I should have" or "Why didn't I?". I decided that a diminished life was not what I would accept, that I had to take the responsibility to build the new life I wanted, to keep what was useful and positive, and discard the negative damaging thoughts and anger.

It was approximately two-and-a-half years later that Christopher Lubamba was finally sentenced to 65 years' imprisonment, with an effective 33 years to serve. A number of other victims also came forward to help remove him from society. By taking full responsibility for my responses, I chose not to hate him. If I had, he would have continued to have an influence over my life and I would continually be cast in the role of his victim.

Those 15 minutes in 1999 were significant only in that they were the catalyst to create the person I am, and the life I have now. When I tell people about my experiences they say that I am brave, balanced and strong, they are amazed that I am not bitter, angry or diminished because that is what society expects, allows and even condones. I have certainly been furious, shattered and cynical, I wouldn't be normal if I hadn't, but I didn't want to stay that way, there was no relief in being toxic like that. I have come to realize that I am all I have and I was not willing to have that special uniqueness put out of my sphere of influence and permanently damaged at the whim of someone else. I have never been one to blame others for my circumstance and I mean to continue thinking that way.

Have you made your own choices?

CHAPTER 2
LIQUID ASSETS

“ *We teach people how to treat us.* ”

WALT DISNEY (1901–66)

In the first Superman movie, Lois Lane asks Superman what he stands for and, quick as a flash, he replies, "Truth, justice and the American way." Although you may not agree with his values, you do have to admit that he was clear about what he stood for and what mattered most to him. Could you do the same? Do you know what you stand for? I hope so, because the answers to these questions make up your values and are the foundation for your decisions.

Jeff Bezos, the founder of Internet book store Amazon. com, spent his time answering these questions and identified his company's values as:

" *Work hard. Have fun. Make history.* "

This helps all employees at Amazon understand how they should behave at work. They only need to ask, "Am I working hard, having fun or helping to make history right now? If not, then why am I doing it?"

As a leader, the solutions to many of your challenges will become clear when you find your true values. Most people never take the time to work these out and they remain confused, so let's take a look at how you can begin to discover your own values.

What is your question?

Everyone has one question that they ask themselves regularly throughout the day and this can hold the key to understanding their values. If you are asking questions that move you towards your desired result, you will be open to receiving an answer. You may have asked the question so often that it's become a natural part of your daily activities and you don't even notice it, but there will be one question that you find yourself asking more than any other. It might be "Why am I here?", "Will I ever find someone to love me?", "What's the point?" or "Why does no one ever listen to me?". Take some time to listen to what your question is, because this will help point you in the direction you want to go.

Albert Einstein regularly listened to his own question and he insisted it was important "not to stop questioning because curiosity has its own reason for existing".

When you have identified your one question, think about the consequences of repeating it so regularly. Does it empower you (some examples may be "How can I make a difference?" or "How can I improve?") If so, that's brilliant. If you continue to ask your question, eventually your subconscious mind will work out an answer. If the question disempowers you ("Why can't I do anything right?" or "Why does it always happen to me?"), then think about changing it to a question that will help you move in the direction you want.

Stanislavsky Lech changed his own question after he had been taken to the Krakow concentration camp, where he had witnessed his family's execution and endured the back-breaking and soul-sapping physical work that all the prisoners had to do. Every day he would wake up, take a look at the hellish conditions and ask himself, "How am I going to survive today?"

One day when he woke up and took his usual look around, he felt an overwhelming sense that he was going to die. He had asked his question so many times that he had run out of answers and death appeared the only option available. When he was faced with this, he decided that he was going to attempt to escape before he gave up his own life and he began changing his question to a more empowering one: "How can I escape?"

Soon afterwards, he smelled the stench of rotting flesh coming from a pile of naked bodies that had been gassed and then piled on top of a truck. He knew that this terrible scene offered an answer to his question. He immediately took off his clothes and lay among the bodies, pretending to be dead. Eventually the truck drove off into the mountains where the bodies were dumped in an open grave. Lech remained there for hours until he was sure that he was safe, before he made his break for freedom 20 miles across the mountains to safety.

What differentiates Lech from the millions who died in the concentration camps? There were obviously several factors, but he believed: "The one critical difference was that I asked a different question, over and over again, always with the expectation of eventually receiving an answer."

What's your question?

What are your values?

Once you know your question, think about the behaviours you need to help you answer it.

When James Timpson had identified that he wanted to build his chain of shoe-repair shops, he identified the values that he wanted his staff to display through the unlikely source of a children's book. He found a simple way of being able to express his values by using pictures of the Mr Men cartoon characters who displayed characteristics that everyone could understand: Mr Happy, Mr Friendly, Mr Keen, Mr Faithful, Mr Prompt, Mr Reliable, Mr Neat, Mr Smart and Mr Skilful.

Timpson explained, "The pictures offer a clear message about how to behave. They don't have to be saints; these are realistic values which anyone can live up to. They are the sort of behaviours which a customer would expect when they visit a shoe repair shop. These are values which are relevant, sustainable and memorable."

What are your own values? Write down as many (or as few) as you can. Be completely honest and don't write down what you would like them to be. There are no right or wrong values. Just list the values that are important to you.

Prioritize them

Rank your list of values in order of their importance to you.

Are they helpful?

Now look at your current values and ask whether they help or hinder you in becoming the leader you want to be.

US billionaire and tycoon Donald Trump offers a great example of this point. Early in his career, he identified that his values included power, risk and success in business. In the mid 1970s, New York City faced bankruptcy and most new property developers were hesitant to make investments in such a precarious climate. Trump decided that he would purchase an old building, which he planned to convert into the Grand Hyatt Hotel. If his values had been about living conservatively and being safety conscious, he clearly wouldn't have made the same decision.

Trump admitted that as his successes grew, he lost sight of these values: "I started to ask 'what can I enjoy owning?' instead of, 'what's the most profitable deal to be made?'" This change in values helped to bring about his spectacular downfall, where he lost most of his estate. When he returned to his original values, he once again enjoyed more dazzling success.

If your values don't fit with who you want to be as a person, it will be impossible to achieve your ultimate vision. Use this opportunity to look at areas that need to be modified to help you. Remember, you are creating the rules to your own game, so use whichever ones fit.

Mother Teresa had the following poem displayed in her office to act as a reminder of her own values and behaviour:

People are often unreasonable, illogical and self centred
Forgive them anyway

If you are kind people may accuse you of selfish ulterior motives
Be kind anyway

If you are successful you will win some false friends and some
*   true enemies*
Succeed anyway

If you are honest and frank, people may cheat you
Be honest and frank anyway

What you spend years building, someone could destroy
* overnight*
Build anyway

If you find serenity and happiness, they may be jealous
Be happy anyway

The good you do today people will often forget tomorrow
Do good anyway

If you give the world your best it may never be enough
Give it your best anyway

You see in the final analysis
It was never between you and them anyway
© *Copyright Kent M. Keith, 1968, 2001.*

For more help on discovering your values, turn to the exercises on page 149.

CHAPTER 3

LIQUID CRYSTAL DISPLAY

" Men wanted for hazardous journey. Small wages. Bitter cold. Long hours of complete darkness. Constant danger. Safe return doubtful. Honour and recognition in the event of success. "

ADVERT PLACED IN *THE TIMES* NEWSPAPER, 1913 BY ERNEST SHACKLETON FOR MEN TO JOIN HIS 1915 ANTARCTIC EXPEDITION.

The above job advert, featured in a national newspaper, still currently holds the record for the most responses. Its success is down to the colourful picture it paints for the reader. It takes you on a journey, which is an essential starting point for a leader.

Although Captain Kirk boasted to the crew of the Starship *Enterprise* that they were going on a journey into the unknown, most people want to have a clear idea about where they're heading. As a leader, if you don't provide this, the chances are that you'll head off into the darkness alone.

Creating a vision must be the first action you undertake, because not only does it set a positive theme for the future, it also gives a clear direction and destination that everyone can move towards. Think of it as the equivalent of the North Star, which the captain of a ship uses to navigate its course. Without it, the future is at best uncertain and at worst perilous. A quote from the Bible (Proverbs 19: 8) neatly summarizes the importance of this point: "Where there is no vision, the people perish."

Walt Disney had a vision that continued to remain bright and attractive to him right up to the day he died. In 1966, he was seriously ill and suffering from lung cancer and he was unable to move from his hospital bed. Despite his condition, one young journalist was still so persistent in requesting an interview with him that eventually Disney ignored the advice of his doctors and agreed to meet him.

Disney was only able to talk in a hoarse whisper and so the journalist had to lie next to him on the bed to ask his questions about the plans he had for building a theme park called Disneyland. Despite his being racked with pain, the journalist later described how Walt "lit up" with delight and excitement while he painted an imaginary map of the park on the ceiling above his head. He was able to point out where the various buildings and attractions would be and described in rich, colourful detail the sights, sounds, tastes, smells and feelings every visitor would be able to experience when they stepped through the gates of his magical world.

The journalist remarked that his lasting memory of the interview was the clarity of this dying man's vision of Disneyland. It was no surprise that even though Disney died shortly after the interview, the power of his vision moved so many others that work continued on the park for another six years until Disneyland eventually became a reality.

Does your vision have similar power?

Studies indicate that most people want to believe that they are working towards an interesting and compelling future. An annual survey is conducted among the world's leading 200 companies, which focuses on what motivates employees. Both leaders and employees complete the survey and list their top ten motivating factors. Every year, "having a clear vision" is in the employees' top three. (Worryingly, leaders consistently tend to rank "having a clear vision" in tenth place!)

So how do you go about creating a vision that both you and your team can readily embrace?

First of all, let's take a look at the opposite of vision.

A vision is not a short-term fix

Take care not to mistake a short-term goal for a vision. A vision needs to be far more long-term, sustainable, memorable and distinctive than that. Don't create a vision for what you will do today or tomorrow, but think about what you will create in a year or two. By doing this, you can begin to create a long-term and long-lasting future.

There is a term, "marketing myopia", which was first coined in the 1960s and which illustrates this point perfectly.

Theodore Levitt, a famed academic, wrote a *Harvard Business Review* case on the death of the kerosene oil industry in the early twentieth century, and tried to understand how it had gone from being one of the world's most powerful and wealthiest industries to becoming virtually extinct so quickly. The findings suggested that the leaders of the industry had suffered from marketing myopia and had not invested enough time in creating a long-term vision for their business. They believed that they were in the kerosene industry and as long as they continued to keep on doing what they did, they would continue to remain successful.

Instead, if they had taken the time to look forward and visualize their long-term future, they would have recognized that they were, in fact, part of the illumination industry (the kerosene was used to light oil lamps) and so when cheaper, cleaner methods of illuminating a house emerged with the advent of gas and electricity, the leaders were not in a position to adapt and evolve. If they had created a longer-term vision, the chances are that they would have been leading the change to gas and electricity use.

Levitt's study suggested a number of other industries that struggled because they were too short term in their visions. The railways struggled because they considered themselves to be in the railway industry rather than the transportation business. In the 1930s Hollywood slumped for a while because it remained convinced that it was in the movie business and not popular entertainment. If they had got it right, the leaders of the railways would have developed cars and planes and Hollywood would have invented television.

Think long-term when creating your vision.

A vision is different from a mission

There is a crucial distinction between the vision and mission. A vision is the dream of what things will be like when you arrive at your chosen destination; the mission is the motivation that will get you there. Think of it like planning a holiday: your vision involves images of you lying on a sun-kissed golden beach with a gentle breeze blowing and a large cocktail positioned next to your sun lounger; your mission for the holiday is to relax and unwind for a few weeks and have a break from the stresses of work.

Henry Ford, the founder of the Ford Motor Company, understood this distinction and used a clear vision to capture the imagination of investors in his company. He shared the dream of "building a car for the great multitude. It will be so low in price that no man making a good salary will be unable to own one and enjoy with his family, the blessing of hours in God's great open spaces. The horse will have disappeared from our highways, the automobile will be taken for granted and we will give a large number of men employment at good wages."

Note that he didn't share how he was going to build the car and what the specific cost would be.

A vision should set out to capture the wow, not the how.

A vision shouldn't contain lots of facts and figures

Your vision doesn't have to contain lots of hard data, such as costs, amounts and volumes. This doesn't mean that it lacks substance, but your aim should be to focus on the emotions of the listener rather than their intellect (or wallet!). If you do feel it absolutely necessary to include facts and figures (and I would advise that this should be only *in extremis*), follow the advice of former US President Richard Nixon, who instructed his aides: "Never give me a naked fact. Put it in a little story."

A vision shouldn't be focused on what you don't want

This important point allows me to use a clever-sounding sentence to explain myself, so please indulge me for a moment. Here goes . . . Did you know that it is impossible for your brain to process a negative in your neurology?

Phew! Thanks for allowing me that. Now, what do I mean by it?

Stop reading for a moment and *don't*, I repeat *don't*, think about an elephant wearing a pink tutu and dancing the can-can.

What did you just think of? That's right, a dancing elephant.

When creating your vision, you need to pay careful attention to this aspect. The vision shouldn't contain what you don't want or what you want to avoid. First, nobody will be inspired by it; secondly, and more importantly, they will automatically start to focus on the very things you want them to avoid. They can't help this. It's in their neurology.

Think like racing drivers do. When they are going to crash, despite all of their instincts screaming at them to look at the wall where the car is heading, they are trained to look away from it and focus back on the track. They understand that by focusing on where they want to be, they greatly increase their chances of avoiding a crash. Don't make your vision into the equivalent of the wall.

At that point we will swerve away from what a vision should not be and focus instead on what great visions should include.

A vision must be exciting

When Sir Richard Branson decided that Virgin was going to branch out from the music business and into airlines, his closest advisers told him that he was risking making a big mistake. Experts warned that he had no idea how the airline industry worked and cautioned him about the dangers of moving away from his area of expertise. He outlined a vision to his staff that included the reassurance: "We are not going into the airline industry. We are still remaining in the entertainment industry, only at 30,000 feet."

His exciting vision reassured those who doubted him, and attracted people who had never worked in the travel

35

industry before to want to join him, because they could understand what he wanted to achieve. There are now legendary stories of Virgin crew members singing the safety instructions to passengers; these people understood the vision. Branson's airline has subsequently gone from strength to strength and Virgin Atlantic has been "Airline of the Year" a record five consecutive times.

Southwest Airlines, the world's most successful airline company and the only one to record an annual profit in each of its 30 years in business, has an equally meaningful vision. If you were to ask one of its employees about the company's vision, the chances are that you'd receive a response including the phrase that it is in "the freedom business". Southwest's overall vision is to "democratize the skies" and allow people on a budget to be able to visit their family and friends.

Such visions allow employees to see beyond the routine demands of their jobs and feel that they are involved in something exciting.

A vision should be true and consistent with what you stand for

It is easy to write a future vision that is so far removed from the current reality that it is unrecognizable. You must ensure that your vision remains true to and consistent with your values and behaviour, otherwise it will immediately lose any credibility.

There is a famous example of a large multinational company in America that spent millions of dollars taking its leaders to country retreats, where they could work out a vision for their business. In the vision, they included the kind of behaviours they wanted to see everyone in the company demonstrating on a daily basis. These included:

- communication

- respect

- integrity

- excellence

These all sound very noble and worthy – until you know that the company was Enron, whose leaders were proven to have behaved in exactly the opposite manner.

How credible does their vision sound now?

A vision must be credible

This is a similar point to the last one, but if you are looking for people to make an emotional commitment, it's important that your vision is believable. If not, you risk provoking a mixture of disbelief, cynicism and resentment by trying to stretch the boundaries of realism too far.

Take Bob Dylan, who experienced this kind of backlash. In the 1960s he assumed the role of the poetic voice of the anti-establishment movement in America. He had the folk world at his feet, as his thoughtful melodies seemed to capture feelings and hearts. Suddenly, without any warning, he attempted to create a new vision for himself by appearing at a concert backed by a rock band and trying to reinvent himself as a rock star. For many of his fans this was a leap beyond what they considered to be believable. A famous four-word review of his next album by the critic Marcus Griel was: "What is this shit?"

Dylan did go on to reinvent himself and gain iconic status within the music world, but many of his original fans still feel betrayed by the fact that he attempted to create a vision that they couldn't believe in and that he left them behind. Don't make the same mistake with your vision by offering a future that's inconceivable to your followers.

A vision should be persuasive

Remember, the purpose of creating a vision is to persuade other people to join you willingly on the journey, so they must be able to see a successful and rewarding future for themselves. When crafting your vision, consider your audience and whether it will actually achieve this for them.

Mother Teresa was lauded for her humanitarian efforts and she understood the power of a persuasive vision as well as anyone. As a young Catholic nun she left Albania to teach the children of wealthy expatriates in Calcutta. One day, when she was out walking, she stopped and tended to a beggar, who subsequently died in her arms. She later reflected, "I had seen the fear in his eyes that he would never be loved and I saw that this fear appeared to be shared by lots of others." She left the school, established her Missions of Charity and found thousands of other people who wanted to share her vision of attempting to remove that fear from the eyes of the poor – to let them experience being loved.

Mother Teresa's vision wasn't limited to the poor of India. In 1986 she visited a maximum security prison in New York and met inmates who had contracted AIDS. She claimed to immediately recognize the same look in their eyes as the one she saw daily on the streets of Calcutta. When she met Edward Koch, the mayor of New York, she persuaded him to open America's first AIDS centre. She did this by recognizing that she needed to create a vision that was persuasive to Koch.

She told him that he had a huge part to play in setting an example to the world. She said, "You may feel that what you do is just a drop in the ocean but if that drop was not in the ocean, I believe that the ocean would be less because of your one missing drop."

Koch later admitted that it was due to "the intensity of this vision, that I was able to make a difference to the lives of others, which bowled me over".

Make sure that your vision speaks to others in the same way.

A vision must be relevant

"What's in it for me?" This is a crucial question that everyone wants an answer to before they commit to make the vision a reality. The less they understand what the benefits to them are, the less their commitment will be.

Sir John Harvey-Jones understood this when he was the leader of chemicals giant ICI. In 1981 the company had recorded its first ever quarterly loss and so the boss worked on creating a compelling vision of ICI in the future, which included becoming the first company to reach a billion-pound profit. He clearly outlined a vision where his people would benefit by being associated with this impressive achievement. The vision was achieved within two years.

Sir John reflected, "The real power in the vision lay in it being both a 'first' for any equivalent UK company and by also including the word 'billion', as this would strike a chord in the minds of the press, the analysts and, most importantly, the company's people."

A vision must be easily understandable

The former US secretary of state Colin Powell challenges leaders by suggesting that "if you can't explain what you are doing to your mother, maybe you don't really understand it", which is a good rule of thumb to follow and will prevent you from trying to be too clever.

This is not to suggest that your mum is stupid, quite the opposite. Most mums see through any unnecessarily clever and complex terms you're using to get straight to the heart of the matter; all of the best visions are able to achieve this. For example, Martin Luther King didn't stand at the Washington Monument and use complicated jargon like "I have a critical path schedule" to bring about the civil rights revolution. He chose powerfully simple images of "the red hills of Georgia" being the backdrop for "little black boys and girls holding hands with little white boys and girls".

Equally, John F Kennedy didn't challenge his people to "strengthen the moon programme" or "create strategic alliances to uncover possible synergies". He simply said,

"This nation should commit itself to achieving the goal, before this decade is out, of landing a man on the moon and returning him safely to earth." What is there not to understand about that?

If you can't manage to achieve simplicity through the power of your words, think about how you can achieve it through imagery instead.

Walt Disney created a team of Imagineers to come up with new and exciting creations for his studios and theme parks and this group is still a much-valued part of the organization. One of their ideas was Animal Kingdom, which was an improvement on the traditional zoo. The Imagineers attended the various meetings and shared the vision of their Animal Kingdom with the board members, who repeatedly rejected it because they were unable to understand just how it could be so exciting.

Rather than get frustrated, the Imagineers decided to bring some realism into the theoretical and intellectual debate and brought along a 400 lb Bengal tiger to the next board meeting. Suddenly, the long discussions about whether animals were exciting enough stopped. The Animal Kingdom got the green light and enjoyed its $1 billion opening in 1998.

How can you make your vision come alive?

A vision must make you go "wow!"

Sir Laurence Olivier once responded to a young Albert Finney's question about how he could visualize being successful on the stage. Olivier considered the question before he proclaimed, "Do what I do, dear boy, amaze yourself with your own daring!"

Don't aim to make your vision something that's "okay" or "quite good". Instead, aim to follow Olivier's advice and amaze yourself enough to feel a sense of "wow!".

One of the best visions I have witnessed coming to fruition is the Harlem Children's Zone, a charity that looks after children in deprived areas of New York. They outlined their own powerful vision in the form of a poem, which captures the real essence of their work.

Maybe before we didn't know
That Corey is afraid to go
To school, the store, to roller-skate
He cries a lot for a boy of eight.
But now we know each day is true
That other girls and boys cry too.
They cry for us to lend a hand.
Time for us to make a stand.

And little Maria's window screen
Keeps out flies and other things
But she knows to duck her head,
When she prays each night 'fore bed
Because in the window comes some things
That shatter little children's dreams.
For some, the hour glass is out of sand.
Time for us to make a stand.

And Charlie's deepest, secret wishes
Is someone to smother him with kisses
And squeeze and hug him tight, so tight,

When he pretends to put up a fight
Or at least someone to be home
Who misses him, he's so alone.
Who allowed this child-forsaken land?
Look in the mirror and take a stand.

And on the Sabbath, when we pray
To our God, we often say,
'Oh Jesus, Mohammed, Abraham,
I come to better understand
How to love and give,
And live the life you taught to live.'
In faith we must join hand-in-hand
Suffer the children? Take a stand!

And tonight, some child will go to bed,
No food, no place to lay their head.
No hand to hold, no lap to sit,
To give slobbery kisses from slobbery lips
So you and I must succeed
In this crusade, this holy deed,
To say to the children in this land:
Have hope. We're here. We take a stand!

Geoffrey Canada, February 14 1996.

Go to page 150 for further exercises on how you can create a powerful vision.

Fergus Finlay

Fergus Finlay was the chef de cabinet of the Irish Labour Party and is now the chief executive of the charity Barnardo's in Ireland. He also writes a weekly column for the Irish Examiner *and is the author of a number of bestselling books. He previously served as an adviser to Dick Spring from 1983 to 1997. During this time he was involved in campaigns that led to the election of Mary Robinson as the first female Labour president, the large increase in the number of Labour Teachta Dálas (MPs) in 1992 and the dropping of the constitutional ban on divorce in 1996. Fergus also worked in government as press secretary in the 1980s and helped to bring the Special Olympics Games to Ireland in 2003, the world's biggest sporting event that year.*

When my daughter Mandy, who has Down's Syndrome, was born, the doctor who delivered her coldly announced that she wouldn't cause us much trouble but that she would never amount to much either. She has spent the rest of her life proving him wrong – on both counts!

We were thrilled in 1995 when she became the first member of our family to be chosen to represent her country. She had been selected as a member of the Irish basketball team who were competing at the World Special

Olympic Games in New Haven, Connecticut and we decided that we would extend our mortgage to go out to America to support her.

The Special Olympics movement – for intellectually disabled athletes – was founded in the 1960s by Eunice Kennedy Shriver, John F Kennedy's sister. The World Games had always been staged in America and it had consistently been a great and wonderful event. It was clear, however, that the organization wasn't as good as it could be; the accommodation, the catering and traffic management were all pretty poor. Mary Davis, who was Director of Special Olympics in Ireland, was there, and we agreed with each other that if we ever got the chance, we could do at least as good a job in Ireland, if not better. She agreed with me.

At this time, I was working in Irish politics, as an adviser to the deputy prime minister, Dick Spring, who was also serving as foreign minister. Shortly after we got back home to Ireland, my wife Frieda and I had an opportunity to meet with Eunice Kennedy Shriver and her husband, Sargent Shriver, because Eunice's sister was serving as the US ambassador to Dublin. With our fingers crossed behind our backs during the meeting, I suggested that Ireland would make a great job of hosting the Games. I had a very clear vision about what we could achieve and I shared it with them. We explained that we wanted to use the Games as a vehicle for raising awareness about intellectual disability through showcasing the ability of our athletes.

I knew from my own experience in America that the Special Olympic Games can be very inspirational and I wanted as many people as possible to experience this. However, we also knew that we would have to create an event that would capture the public's imagination – if it wasn't a success we risked setting back the cause of awareness.

I explained to Eunice that the government and Irish society would get right behind it, and that it would not cost the movement anything. During the conversation, Eunice revealed that they were very keen to "internationalize" the World Games and they agreed, almost immediately, to put it out to tender and allow countries to bid for the right to host it.

I genuinely felt that given half a chance Ireland could really put on a great event, and Mary Davis and I agreed that we should be aiming at a lasting legacy too. After this initial meeting I had to win others over and I started with my own boss, Dick Spring. He helped to persuade the government of the day to commission a study – what the logistics were, what additional sports facilities would be needed to stage the World Games, how we would coordinate and manage traffic, accommodation and catering for the 5000 to 7000 athletes and a similar number of family visitors as well as worldwide media, and thousands of Irish participants. A small team, led by some senior civil servants, drew up the feasibility study and we made this the basis of our bid for the Games. The government also agreed to put up €5 million in seed capital to underpin it.

Eventually, the tendering process was whittled down to Argentina and Ireland, and when the team assessing the bids came to Ireland we persuaded the government to host them. It was a great moment when Ireland was finally confirmed as the 2003 host country.

At this point, we had about four years to prepare. It was important to recognize that we needed the best people in the right positions and so we persuaded a leading businessman, Denis O'Brien, to chair the Games organizing committee. Mary Davis was appointed director. She and Denis quickly established a strong working relationship – both had huge skills individually and quickly arrived at a point where "the whole was greater than the sum of the parts" – in which their teamwork, and the work of the bigger team they built around them, brought real added value to the preparations for the Games.

From the very beginning, they decided to set their sights high. They wanted U2 to perform at the opening ceremony and to have Nelson Mandela declare the Games officially open in front of 75,000 people at Dublin's Croke Park. In the end, it took a team of several hundred full-time staff to pull it all together. One of the lessons in managing so many people, most of them working under pressure all the time, was that messages had to be clear and direct.

When we began to communicate our vision for the Games, we knew that we were capturing the public imagination because people quickly began to sign up as volunteers. In the end we had 30,000 volunteers! We soon realized that we were going to need very large venues just to train them.

At the same time, we were preparing a host town programme, where towns and villages in Ireland were paired up with participating countries. Those countries would send their athletes to that town for a week's orientation in advance of the Games. All over Ireland, North and South, towns clamoured to join the programme and get involved. We were ultimately able to accommodate 150 nationalities and most teams were welcomed with parties, gifts, local celebrities and much more.

During this period of frenetic activity, particularly through watching Mary and Denis, I learned a valuable lesson about leadership: you have to keep really focused on your objectives and the outcomes you want. Keeping your vision in mind throughout is essential. If you don't, it's easy to become distracted and to lose sight of the end goal. This approach helped to ensure that there was never any real doubt that the Games would be a great success.

I can't remember in great detail how I felt when it all came together as I was crying too hard! There was, however, one moment I do remember that made it all worthwhile. It sounds like a silly thing now, but I had persuaded Calor Gas to supply the fuel and the lighting mechanism for the Olympic flame. The lighting of the flame is, naturally, the highlight of the opening ceremony and a lot of preparation had been carried out beforehand to ensure that the athletes applying the torch to the cauldron would cause a flame to shoot up to light a giant bowl. If that hadn't worked, I would have felt personally responsible for spoiling the key moment of the ceremony.

I will never forget the feeling of exhilaration when it all worked perfectly and when Pierce Brosnan came on stage as James Bond to introduce U2, who brought Nelson

Mandela on with them. There wasn't a dry eye in the stadium!

I watched the whole of the opening ceremony from the comfort of a box, which afforded us a great view. It seemed fitting that the whole family, who had all been present in Connecticut when the idea was born, gathered together to share the completion of a long journey. (The only exception was my daughter Vicky, who had worked full-time as part of the organizing team of the opening ceremony and spent the evening on the pitch.)

This was the last – and possibly the most important – leadership lesson I learned from the whole incredible experience. When you decide to pursue your vision, make sure that you enjoy it!

CHAPTER 4

SAILING BY THE NORTH STAR

" Where are we going lads? To the toppermost of the poppermost! "

JOHN LENNON (1940–80)

There is a very good chance that when you reach this chapter you give some serious thought to skipping it. Mission statements are often full of nonsense and are completely and utterly irrelevant.

Barry Gibbons, the former head of Burger King, captured this experience when he started working for the company. He arrived at the headquarters and found that the only piece of paper left in his office was the old mission statement hanging on his wall. "It was so full of crap and humbug," he said, "that there and then, I invented a new word to describe the language normally used in mission statements: 'crumbug.'"

Missions are often derided, but that doesn't mean that leaders shouldn't give the company's mission their full attention. Essentially, you should help people to understand why they do what they do.

A recent survey estimated that nearly 65 per cent of the population don't know why they bother to go to work, beyond doing it for the money, but research indicates that the 35 per cent who have identified a clear purpose are up to eight times more effective. Other tests show that those with a purpose are more likely to be happier and suffer less illness and absence than those who live their lives without one. Yet still most leaders either ignore missionsor instead waste time creating crumbug statements that mean little to those they are aimed at.

Don't be one of them!

Here is an incredible example from the world of computer games, which further justifies spending time understanding your own mission. Most games tend to follow a consistent pattern where the majority of sales take place within the first six months of release and then quickly dip as players move on to the latest new offering. There is one game, however, which has managed to break this pattern: The Sims. It keeps selling in record numbers and is played by the widest range of people. In fact, more than half of the game's players are teenage girls, who are the least likely group to play computer games.

If you're not familiar with The Sims, the idea is that a player is responsible for every aspect of the lives of the character they create. They can decide the sex, the beauty and even the character's hairstyle. However, a large number of players of the original game gave the feedback that this game soon became boring because it lacked any real purpose. They said that although you could create the perfect family, there was no greater meaning to it. They compared the game to eating Chinese food – at first it satisfies you, but you're soon hungry again. In short, without a mission, they got bored.

The creators therefore made amendments to the game and included a mission for every player, which ranged from getting a job through to getting married. Fulfilling the mission helped the player gain points, which allowed the Sim character to begin earning money, to get fit and to become fashionable. By adding a mission, the game became even more popular and has continued to defy the traditional sales trends.

Great sports leaders have long understood the importance of identifying a mission with which all of the players can identify. For example, Sir Clive Woodward tried to find a mission for his England rugby team that would stop the players being concerned only with their own individual performances, and instead start to focus on how to make the team successful at international tournaments. After a great deal of debate, he identified that the mission of the entire team, from the coaches through to the administration staff and the players, was "to inspire the nation". This became the banner under which they all gathered and it was their mantra until they finally achieved it by winning the World Cup in 2003 and truly inspired the whole nation.

Sir Alex Ferguson uses a similar approach in maintaining Manchester United at the forefront of domestic footballing success. At the start of every season, he gives a speech to his players in which he describes the club as being like "a bus that never stops moving forward". He challenges his players to keep improving and raising their standards to ensure "that they remain on the bus", which will continue to move on without them. The potency of this message is such that Eric Cantona, one of Ferguson's most influential players, describes ten years after he retired how powerful it was: "We stayed strong because we were all on the same bus and we all felt in danger. We worked together to survive and when you quit, you don't have that any more. There is nothing as intense as this feeling of sharing a mission which Ferguson instils."

John Lennon knew the importance of a mission when the Beatles first began. They had been dismissed by Decca Records, who believed that "groups of guitars were on their way out", and so he identified their purpose and said, "I started this thing where I would shout out 'Where are we going lads?' And they'd shout, 'To the toppermost of the poppermost!' We carried on working on being the best band that night. After that we wanted to be the best in the Cavern and after that the best in Liverpool."

Great business leaders also understand the power of identifying a powerful purpose. My favourite example relates to when Rich Teerlink was running the Harley-Davidson motorbike company. He spent a long time trying to convince Wall Street investors that it was not a motorbike manufacturer but was instead a company selling experiences. He finally managed to convince them by sharing the company's mission. It was: "To sell the ability to a 43-year-old accountant to dress in black leather, ride through small towns and have people be afraid of him."

How could you not remember a mission like that?

Let's now look at the two laws that will help you to clarify your own great mission.

Meaning

First of all, it must be relevant to you. Victor Frankl, an Austrian psychologist who survived being a prisoner at the Auschwitz concentration camp, recognized this fact: "Everyone has their own specific mission in life to carry out. Everyone's task is as unique as is their opportunity to implement it." Frankl made it his own mission to survive the camp's horrors and teach mankind how to avoid ever allowing such atrocities to be repeated.

Don't just list what you think sounds good or noble, but take the time to identify what your meaning is. An effective mission should focus on what it would mean to successfully achieve it and embody it.

A journalist once chased Indian leader Gandhi through a busy train station, hoping to get an interview for his newspaper. Despite the man's impressive persistence, Gandhi politely declined to respond to his questions. Finally, as the train was pulling out of the station, the reporter called out: "Please give me a message for the people!" Without hesitation, Gandhi leaned out of the window and shouted back, "My life is my message!"

Is your mission something you can exhibit every day?

Apply a bit of former US President Bill Clinton's thinking (no, not that sort!) to test whether the mission carries any meaning for others. Clinton was a master of connecting to the US public, which voted him in for two terms despite his indiscretions. A great example of this came in 1996, when he attended a live televised debate with Republican Presidential candidate Bob Dole. It was all very structured and both men were positioned behind their lecterns.

When the first question came in, it challenged each of them to answer what their legacy would be as President. Dole went first and delivered his obviously well-rehearsed answer in a polished and slick manner. When it was Clinton's turn to answer, he said nothing but walked from behind his lectern to the front of the audience, looked the man who had asked the question straight in the eye and started his answer by using the man's name.

Game, set and match; presidency.

Imagine looking into the eyes of your team and explaining how your mission is meaningful to each of them. If you can't, maybe the mission's not right.

Avoid relying on corporate sound bites and clichés, but create the mission from your heart. When Winston

Churchill was elected Prime Minister and asked to lead his country through the war, he stood before the nation and declared, "I have nothing to offer you but my blood, toil, tears and sweat." Imagine if he was required to make this same powerful mission statement today. It would be stripped of all emotion and put into a company-approved PowerPoint presentation:

> My offer:
> - Blood
> - Toil
> - Sweat
> - Tears

It loses something, doesn't it?

T-shirt law

"Frankie Says Relax."

Come on, own up. Who will admit to having a T-shirt sporting that message during the early 1980s, the decade fashion forgot? Think about how memorable an image or a short sentence can be. The Coliseum in Rome gets just 1 per cent of the number of tourists who visit the Leaning Tower of Pisa each year because they are drawn there by the simple image of the tower.

However, there is a critical message for all leaders in this simple slogan. It is a great example of the T-shirt law.

The T-shirt law states that on the front of any T-shirt you can only get one picture or message. When you have identified your mission, ruthlessly edit it until it can be emblazoned across a T-shirt. If you can't, it's still too complicated.

This isn't particularly easy, but it is absolutely necessary. Churchill understood this rule and once wrote a long letter to his wife, Clementine, which ended with the apology, "I am sorry I wrote such a long letter, I did not have time to write a short one."

Trailers for Hollywood films are a great example of how the essence of a film can be boiled down to fit the T-shirt law.

- "The general who became a slave. The slave who became a gladiator. The gladiator who defied an emperor." (*Gladiator*)

- "Mischief. Mayhem. Soap." (*Fight Club*)

- "An adventure 65 million years in the making." (*Jurassic Park*)

- "Collide with destiny." (*Titanic*)

Some companies successfully condense their mission down to just two words. Phil Knight, the founder of Nike, has a simple mission that is etched into the brains of all who work at the company's Oregon offices: "Crush Reebok!" Pepsi and Coca-Cola also have similar two-word missions aimed at defeating the other.

Before you begin to identify your own mission, try this little competition. I want you to spot the real missions from the ones that I've made up.

1. "Our challenge is to efficiently revolutionize competitive services and continually disseminate diverse opportunities while promoting personal employee growth."

2. "The customer can count on us to interactively leverage others' value-added meta-services in order that we may synergistically simplify high standards in technology."

3. "Our clients can count on us to professionally leverage existing multimedia-based products in order that we may collaboratively administrate ethical content for 100 per cent customer satisfaction."

4. "Total quality, efficiency, service, performance, dedication, utilization, domination. We stand for virtually nothing less."

5. "As ambitious employees of our budding corporation, we, as a whole, shall aim to affordably manufacture the highest quality products that will exponentially increase mankind's eternal quest for a higher worldwide standard of living."

6. "Our company is dedicated to epitomizing the zenith of achievement. Furthermore, our commitment to excellence surpasses that of our competitors. When one seeks to climb the mountain of greatness, he cannot stumble over the cliff of expense. For this

reason we seek not to achieve the paradigm of success. We seek to embody it."

The answer is that the first three are false. Scarily, the last three are all genuine company mission statements.

Finally, let's look at some great mission statements.

Bayern Munich FC: More than 1–0

The football club Bayern Munich has the nickname "FC Hollywood" because it is renowned for employing superstar players and is involved in gossip column scandals as regularly as football matters.

A number of years ago, however, the club revised its mission and came up with a simple message that is applicable to everybody associated with the club, from the players through to the fans. It wanted to be a club that was more than just about results; it wanted to stand for something in the community and among its followers; it also wanted to be a club that looked to entertain as opposed to merely winning by the bare minimum.

Since Bayern Munich adopted the mission, it has won a European Cup and three consecutive domestic titles.

Waldorf Astoria Hotel: Creating customers for life

One stormy night, many years ago, an elderly man and his wife entered the lobby of a small hotel in Philadelphia. Trying to get out of the rain, the couple approached the desk and hoped to get a room. The clerk, a friendly young man, explained that there were three conventions in town and all the rooms were taken. However, he refused to allow the guests to head back out into the night and offered them his own room instead.

Two years later, the young clerk received a letter from the old man with a return ticket to New York. He was invited to come to the city, where the old man led him to the corner of 5th Avenue and 34th Street and pointed to a great new building, a palace of reddish stone with turrets rising into the sky. "That," he said, "is the hotel I have built for you to manage."

The old man was William Waldorf Astor and the hotel was named after him, the original Waldorf Astoria Hotel. The young clerk, George C Bokit, became its first manager and he insisted that all his staff understood the purpose of the hotel, which was to "create customers for life".

Southwest Airlines: To democratize the skies

There are lots of ways in which airlines can compete: in-flight service, loyalty schemes, convenient schedules, route network, leg room, on-board entertainment, quality of food and wine, airport lounges, sleeper beds, punctuality, choice of airport and quality of connections.

Herb Kelleher, the founder of Southwest Airlines, has a simple response to all these competitive challenges: low cost, low cost, low cost, low cost, low cost, low cost, low cost, low cost, low cost, low cost and low cost.

This is very simple, very focused and very effective. Everyone, including the customer, understands what this means for them. The airline keeps cost low to ensure that anyone, whatever their budget, can afford to fly with it, and therefore it truly democratizes the skies.

What is your own mission?

For some further help and ideas as to how you can identify your own mission, turn to page 152.

CHAPTER 5

DRIP EFFECT

> " *Words can be short and easy to speak. Get them right and their echo can be endless.* "
>
> MOTHER TERESA

You've done the exercises at the back of the book and you now have a vision that is positively dripping with colour, feeling and emotion. You have seen the promised land and you are going to get there!

Well, hold on a minute. We need to consider what you do next.

Sir Alf Ramsey, England's World Cup winning manager, was once asked about the secret of great coaching and how he was able to get his players to fully understand his vision of how he wanted the game to be played. His reply sums up a lesson that you need to consider for your own vision:

Constant repetition gets the message home.

Constant repetition gets the message home.

Constant repetition gets the message home.

Constant repetition gets the message home.

Constant repetition gets the message home.

Constant repetition gets the message home.

The 60 per cent rule

As a leader, there is one simple rule that you must bear in mind whenever you go out to share your vision: the 60 per cent rule.

It actually applies to all forms of communication. Whenever you pass information on to others, whether it is sharing your vision or what you did at the weekend, a maximum of only 60 per cent of your message ever gets through to the listener.

Rudolph Guiliani, the former mayor of New York City, learned this lesson quickly after the attacks on 11 September 2001. He took every possible opportunity to reinforce the message to the city's shell-shocked residents that they would recover from the attacks stronger and better. He summed up his approach by explaining, "You don't inform, you over-inform."

You need to over-inform not because people are stupid, but because they have got plenty of other things on their minds. Their children's exams, their holidays, the upcoming visit from the mother-in-law are all thoughts competing for their attention as well as what you are saying.

The 60 per cent rule has long been understood by advertisers, who coined the old maxim "The customer has to see an advert at least six times before they will even start to remember it". Use the same approach when you start to communicate your vision and don't be too subtle in your approach. Even if you have to repeat the same message many times to the same group, don't assume that everyone will remember it. Apply the 60 per cent rule. Repeat the vision again and again and again and again and again . . .

Think about being creative in repeating your vision and consider using stories and myths, which can be incredibly powerful methods of drawing people in and getting your message to stick. Look at all of the world's major religious texts, from the Bible to the Koran. They all use metaphors, stories and analogies to get their message across and this isn't a coincidence.

Ingvar Kamprad, the founder of home furnishing retailer Ikea and the fourth-richest man in the world, appreciates this and has deliberately allowed stories to grow and circulate about him that help to reinforce his vision. He regularly travels to the airport by bus and only ever stays in cheap motels rather than luxurious five-star hotels when he is on business. This simple story is consistent with his vision, which is to "help create a better life for many people by providing cheap but quality furniture for their homes". The anecdote shows a man who is still in touch with reality and is still concerned with getting the best value for money. His bus trips are a metaphor for his company's journey.

Think about how your everyday activities can re-emphasize your vision effectively. Stelios Haji-Ioannou, founder of the discount airline easyJet, begins his meetings by asking his staff to stand behind their chairs. He then asks each of them to tell him whether the chair in front of them is empty or not. The obvious reply is: "Of course it's empty." Stelios then reminds staff of his company's vision, which centres around offering cheap flights and is dependent on planes being full. He uses their responses to remind them that they must focus their efforts on "putting bums on seats".

Fred Smith, the founder of delivery service FedEx, thought that his vision of delivering parcels lacked any real drama, so he revised it to include the idea of a "golden package". Any package the company delivers could be the golden one that transforms a client's business or brings happiness to a family. Suddenly, the need to deliver every package overnight and on time really meant something to every FedEx employee. The company even introduced speed-walking training for all drivers, to reinforce the vision and create a sense of urgency and importance to everyone.

Bill Sweetenham, one of the world's finest swimming coaches, even uses breakfast times to emphasize his message "that success in life is made up of 80 per cent attitude and 20 per cent ability". He insists that a "barnyard breakfast" – a plate of bacon and eggs – is available to all of his swimmers when they sit down to eat, as it helps them to think about the animals that have helped produce the food. The chicken has been involved in producing the egg, while the pig has been fully committed to providing the bacon! Sweetenham then challenges his swimmers to decide whether they are going to be involved in or committed to the day's training session.

The spy writer John le Carré suggests that "a desk is a dangerous place from which to view the world". Ultimately, communicating your vision and mission is all about getting out and about and repeating them as often and as imaginatively as you possibly can.

Turn to page 153 for further ideas on this chapter.

CHAPTER 6
WATER GAUGE

"In preparing for battle, I have always found that plans are useless but analysis and planning are indispensable."

GENERAL DWIGHT D EISENHOWER (1890–1969)

Remember when you were a kid and you would ask your parents to measure your height every few weeks and then keep a record of it by making a mark on the wall? The mark let you know how much you had grown and how fast you were progressing.

This is good training for a skill that all leaders need to develop: keeping a visible measure of progress.

This is obvious stuff, I know, but just consider how you currently analyse and keep score of your progress and whether or not it includes some of the following lessons.

Small details = big answers

Too often when we set off towards our destination we are focused on the big picture, and we can miss answers or obvious shortcuts along the way.

There is a 30-second film made by Harvard psychologists which emphasizes this point. The film concerns six basketball players: three of them are wearing white T-shirts whilst the other three are wearing black T-shirts. The people in white T-shirts have a basketball and, during the film, pass it between one another. Halfway through, a man dressed as a gorilla slowly walks on to the court, saunters through the players, beats his chest in front of the camera and then walks off. Volunteers are asked to watch the film and count the number of times the people in white T-shirts pass the basketball to one another. At the end of the film, when everyone is asked whether they saw anything unusual, amazingly about 80 per cent of viewers fail to spot the gorilla. This is the perfect demonstration of the psychological blind spot we all have.

Ignoring small details, which can often indicate whether we are making progress, is an easy mistake to make. World Cup winner Sir Clive Woodward believes that "winning is a game of inches". Therefore paying attention to the small details will help you reap big rewards. Other great sports leaders understand this as well.

The legendary Australian rugby league coach Wayne Bennett watches closely for tiny, seemingly insignificant details in his training sessions, as he believes that these give clues about where the seeds of victory can be found. For example, he watches running sessions and observes which players ease up when they are two or three yards short of the finish line. He explains that this information "tells me more about the character of my players and how they will react in a tight game than any other information".

Duncan Fletcher, the coach who helped England's cricket team to achieve success after a long period of mediocrity, concurs with this. He recognized that one of his players, Kevin Pietersen, would be a great player by observing the small details. "I saw him drop an easy catch but afterwards, when no one else was watching, I saw him pick himself up and get ready to try again. I knew then that he had the courage and the mental strength to come back from a disaster."

Henry Ford employed similar levels of analysis when he was recruiting executives to work alongside him at his motor company. At dinner time he would watch whether a candidate put salt on their food before tasting it. He viewed this action as a sign of inflexible thinking; after all, if a person wasn't prepared to taste a meal before adding their own changes, this behaviour would transfer to the workplace.

As a business leader you may be aiming to hit your end-of-year sales targets, deliver ambitious annual growth rates or meet your annual cost savings. Take the time to stop and analyse the small stuff along the way. It may contain some big answers.

Identify what is most valuable

In 1906, a young Italian called Wilfredo Pareto was studying wealth and income distribution in nineteenth-century England and he noticed that the majority of land and income (about 80 per cent) was owned by a minority of the population (about 20 per cent). These simple findings ended up making him famous and his very own Pareto Principle became an essential rule for all leaders. It states, quite simply, that 20 per cent of your efforts will produce 80 per cent of your results.

Pareto's discoveries are not reserved to this topic or this particular period of history. It is a universal law. For example, he applied the law when he was gardening and observed that 20 per cent of his pea pods were responsible for 80 per cent of his harvest. Still not convinced? Test the principle for yourself and have a look in your wardrobe. I'll bet that about 20 per cent of your clothes are the ones you wear 80 per cent of the time.

For leaders, the Pareto Principle offers lots of questions that are worth answering. For example, have you identified who your top 20 per cent of customers are? Internet bank Egg did exactly this and discovered that the Pareto Principle was equally applicable to its business. This knowledge allowed its to alter its customer service approach and offer a premium-rate service to its most valuable customers.

Think about your own challenges and how the Pareto Principle can be applied. For example, do you know which 20 per cent of your team consistently deliver 80 per cent of your results? Are you doing enough to keep them feeling motivated and valued?

Applying the 80:20 ratio to your thinking can stop you getting caught up in the whirlwind of daily demands. It can enable you to spot the few really important things that are happening and help focus your energy accordingly.

Instinct

The reason humans, as opposed to other, physically stronger animals, dominate the planet is our ability to reason – to use our intuitive powers to avoid danger.

If an animal is hungry and sees some food with a net hanging over it, the animal will lunge for the food and get caught in the trap. On the other hand, a hungry human will see the food and the net, assess the risk versus the reward of actually getting the food, and intuitively decide against the attempt.

Effective analysis often involves structure, strategies and scientifically proven principles and all these are crucial. Instinct is of equal importance, yet it can often get overlooked.

Your intuition is a blend of instinct, critical thinking and reasoning, common sense and an ability to see the bigger picture. It is your inner voice that always seems to know the right thing to do. Nevertheless, it can easily get snuffed out by your insecurities, your emotional reactions, the demands of your ego, time deadlines and the general stress of trying to compete in the rat race. You should ignore it at your peril.

Brad Gilbert, one of the great tennis coaches, actually teaches his players how to listen to their intuition. He calls it "the DRM approach: Don't Rush Me". He believes that slowing down and carefully listening to that inner voice can be a devastatingly simple but effective weapon. "It will be picking up information which your conscious mind may have missed and will be giving you some powerful data that can aid your way to success," he says. "So tune in to it."

Regular revision

Ten years ago there was an interesting study of how leadership decisions were taken in a number of medium-sized European companies. It showed that two thirds of the major decisions were taken in line with the company's vision and direction. This number dropped to one third when the decisions were regarded as only moderately important. However, only one in twenty of the minor everyday decisions was taken in line with the leaders' vision. Think about the impression this would have on the people working there. Major decisions were taken infrequently, in secret, and were often not made public for good commercial reasons – so they were mostly invisible. The small day-to-day decisions affected everyone and were obvious and public, yet every day people were seeing that the leaders were not true to their vision. It is the small decisions that matter more than large ones to the people who are following you.

Why not consider adopting a simple and obvious practice that will give you a daily reminder to act consistently in line with your vision and values? That was something of which the famous banker J P Morgan paid a small fortune to be reminded.

One day as he was leaving his office, Morgan was approached by a young man who made him an intriguing offer. He said, "I have a formula that guarantees absolute success and I will gladly sell it to you for £25,000." Morgan was curious at this bold statement, but his years of negotiation experience had made him shrewd and suspicious enough to suggest that he be allowed to use the formula on a week's trial. If he judged it to be worthy of the young man's guarantees, he would happily pay the money. The salesman agreed and he handed Morgan an envelope that contained the formula.

One week later, the two men met again and before they had even sat down, Morgan handed over a cheque for £25,000.

The only instructions in the envelope were:

1. Every morning, write a list of things that need to be done that day.

2. Do them.

Ensure that your own to-do list doesn't undermine your vision.

For more ideas on how to become effective at analysing your challenges, turn to page 155.

James Timpson

James Timpson is the managing director of Timpson, a family retail business established in 1865. Timpson trades from 600 sites across the UK and Ireland, has a turnover of more than £100 million and employs 1700 people. The unique upside-down management culture throughout the business ensures that those serving customers are the most important in the business. Timpson has won many awards for both its customer service and its levels of employee satisfaction. Timpson also owns Timpson 24 hr locksmiths, The House Name Plate Company and Keys Direct.

Stelios from easyJet is fond of suggesting that he owes his success in life to being a "lucky sperm" and I suppose that I could class myself in a similar bracket, as I was fortunate enough to be born into a successful family. But there is more to it than that.

My parents have always fostered children and so I have been fortunate to grow up being surrounded by a rich variety of weird and wonderful people, and I have continued to enjoy meeting and dealing with people from all walks of life in my work. When I was a schoolboy, on Saturdays I worked in the family shop in Northwich and loved the banter that went on between the team who worked there. I also enjoyed selling to the general public but above all, I adored the feeling of putting the money away in the till and knowing that I was helping to increase the turnover in the shop. I soon learned that we are all salesmen to some degree. This is an important lesson, which I have carried with me into my leadership roles. Whether you are selling yourself as a leader, your skills or the company you work for, you should always be aware of being visible and that you are on show to others.

During my gap year, between leaving school and starting university, I worked as a relief manager and troubleshooter for the company and learned a lot from this experience. When I went on to Durham University, my eight hours of weekly study left me with plenty of time to work as the area manager in the north east. When I finally left university, however, I was conscious that I wanted to broaden my own experience before I joined the family business on a full-time basis. I wrote to a number of companies and offered them my services, for free, for six months. I ended up working for a company in Gateshead, selling industrial boiler suits. This experience was invaluable, as I found out what it was like to work for crap bosses who didn't care about their staff and I gained an understanding of just how demoralizing this can be, breeding dissatisfaction and unhappiness in the people on the receiving end.

When I eventually joined the family business, my first role was the assistant to the London area manager. We had recently acquired a business where it soon became obvious that many of the staff were stealing from us. I introduced a system, which we still use, called Busman's

Holidays, where we put a star performer into a poorly performing shop and proved just what can be achieved in a week. This is then used as the benchmark to measure the staff in that particular shop afterwards and, in this case, also helped us to prove that money was going missing.

This early experience helped to develop my own leadership values, which are shared by my father, who is the company chairman. We really believe in treating people with decency, respect and loyalty. If you respond to this, we will work hard to look after you. However, if you behave like an arse, we'll treat you as such. These values are instilled throughout the company and we spend nearly £200,000 a year trying to recognize this loyalty through our benefits schemes, which include giving people their birthdays as an extra holiday, access to our hardship fund and visits to our holiday homes. In my experience, this loyalty tends to be repaid many times over.

42 per cent of our staff are recruited through recommendations from our current employees and this approach, of looking to recruit from within our business, is an important factor in our success. The people who work for us really do understand our culture, which is all about empowering the branches to make as much money as possible. We work for the people who are on the shop floor, not the other way around. We have a staff turnover of 14 per cent, which is virtually unheard of in the retail sector (Tesco has an average of 28 per cent), but I believe that this is because we treat people well and trust them to treat us the same way. One simple example of how we do this is through giving every employee the right to spend up to

£500 a week, without any justification, to resolve customer complaints. It is no use having values if you don't support them with your actions.

Good communication is also essential for a leader. I have seen many companies who produce reams and reams of guidelines and brochures about the rules and behaviours they expect, which seem to leave the people they are aimed at feeling confused. I hate rules (I only have two: 1. Put the money in the till and 2. Look the part) and I am constantly working to keep things simple. The biggest-selling newspaper in the UK is *The Sun*, which contains more pictures than words, and I follow a similar approach in my communication style. I use lots of cartoons and fun images to make my points; for example, when we recruit people we use Mr Men cartoons to represent the behaviours we are looking for (Mr Cheerful, Mr Helpful, Mr On-time). We have a ban on people sending memos, as this seems to stop people talking to each other. Problems seem to get solved far quicker this way.

I would suggest that my greatest strength as a leader is my interest in my people. It is something that I would advise other leaders to adopt. We employ over 1700 people in 600 sites in the UK and I try to spend as much time as I can visiting the shops and meeting them. As well as getting to know the gossip, I can understand their challenges and where I can help and support them to be as successful as possible. It also reinforces the message that I am working for them because ultimately, leadership is all about the people who follow you; spending time with them is invaluable. After all, we are all in the people business first; everything else follows after that.

If I could offer you just one lesson about leadership, which I have learned over the years, it is to trust your own gut instinct and then act quickly on it. When you feel that a decision is not right, trust your instinct and act, because you can guarantee that the longer you leave it, the bigger the eventual cost will be. I spend a lot of my time visiting the stores and when I can see that someone is not suited to a job, I move quickly to replace them. This doesn't necessarily mean letting them leave the business, but looking to put them into positions that play to their strengths. For example, we currently have 12 former area managers who were not suited to their roles but who still work for us in other positions that complement their abilities. Their understanding of our business remains vital.

There is a purpose to our business. We are the only shoe-repair business that operates on the high street anywhere in the world. Our approach shouldn't work but it does, and I want to continue building on that success. I imagine that if an alien visiting our world came up with the idea of our business, he would be told off for being ridiculous! I often compare us to a giraffe, because logic suggests that we shouldn't exist but we do, and I keep setting ambitious growth targets to maintain our focus. We will continue to grow our profits to €5 million, then €10, €15 and €20 million eventually.

To achieve this, I need to look after my people and keep them happy, satisfied and motivated. They are our greatest asset and it's critical to treat them that way.

CHAPTER 7
LIQUID SUNSHINE

"" *A leader is a dealer in hope.* ""

NAPOLEON BONAPARTE (1769–1821)

In the 1984 US Presidential elections, Ronald Reagan regularly told a story that left a deep impression on the voters. He compared both himself and his opponent, Walter Mondale, to 5-year-old children. "Mondale," he said, "could be left alone in a room full of toys, but within a few minutes he would become upset after breaking a toy and be scared that he might get into trouble." Reagan, however, suggested that he himself could be left alone in a room full of manure and still have a good time. "With so much manure," he laughed, "I'd believe that there had got to be a pony in there somewhere!"

This characterization of both men, Mondale as a pessimist and Reagan as an optimist, stuck throughout the election campaign and helped Reagan win by a landslide. However, the story contains an important lesson for all leaders. People want their leaders to be optimistic because they offer the hope that problems and obstacles can be overcome. In fact, 19 out of the last 24 US Presidents have all been categorized as optimists.

Ground-breaking research into the motivational impact of hope and optimism was conducted back in 1957 and the results support the idea that these are essential ingredients for all great leaders.

Scientists at Johns Hopkins University in New York conducted an experiment that involved putting rats into a large glass jar filled with water. After a short time, half the rats were momentarily rescued before being put back into the water. The other rats were left to keep swimming. Significantly, the group of rats that had been given a break – and a hope that they would be eventually rescued – continued to swim for more than three days. The group of rats who had not been given a break drowned within hours.

Martin Seligman is a psychologist who has carried out studies on thousands of people, including US Presidents, Olympic gold medallists, politicians and leading business-people. He has found that optimism is an important factor of success.

One experiment that Seligman conducted took place several months before the 1988 Olympic Games in Seoul. The Australian Olympic swimming team completed questionnaires to find out how they viewed problems. One swimmer, Matt Biondi, scored as highly optimistic.

When the swimming team next attended training, the team members were all given fake times that they had recorded during that day's practice. These times meant that they had recorded poor or disappointing performances. They were then asked to get back in the pool and swim again. The swimmers who had been rated as pessimistic recorded even worse swimming times, whereas the swimmers who had been rated as optimistic swam either as well or better. Biondi, the most optimistic, swam the fastest time.

When Biondi went to the Olympic Games, he was widely predicted to win seven gold medals. In his first race he came third. In his next race, he improved slightly to take a silver. The press and the public began to believe that he couldn't cope with the pressure of being a huge favourite. Biondi, however, remained optimistic and did not begin to doubt his own talent. Consequently, he took the gold medal in each of his final five races.

Before we look at how you can improve your ability to be optimistic, it is important to address a few common myths about optimism.

There is an easy way to differentiate between being optimistic and being a wishful thinker. Look for a plan of action. If you can't find one, there is a real danger that wishful thinking is being promoted instead of practical optimism.

Many people make the mistake of studying great achievers, hearing how supremely confident they are about their chances of success and confusing the cause and effect. Tiger Woods, for example, doesn't win because he believes that he will. He believes that he will because he has prepared a plan of action that covers every possible detail to ensure victory.

Jim Stockdale, an American Army officer held as a prisoner of war in Vietnam for over eight years, learned this distinction during that period. Prisoners, who were wishful thinkers, refused to "deal with the brutal reality of prison life" and would set themselves dates on which they believed they would be released. They had no logic or reason for selecting these particular timescales, but the belief that they would come true helped to sustain them for a short period. When the release did not materialize they were crushed and often gave up all hope and "died of a broken heart in prison". In contrast, those who remained optimistic of an eventual release, without "confusing this with a refusal to confront the immediate challenges they were faced with", focused instead on things they could control, such as remaining healthy and mentally active. When the opportunity for release eventually came, they were ready to take it.

Secondly, being an optimist does not require you to become a cross between an evangelist and a children's entertainer. That sort of boundless energy, if it isn't sincere, turns people away from your message. Instead, be true to yourself. For example, Winston Churchill famously hated having his photograph taken and would refuse to smile; he also suffered from dark periods of depression and could never be described as someone who tried to be jolly and upbeat. However, he did embody hope to a beleaguered nation by the manner of his words and, essentially, by being himself.

So how do you become an optimist? There are three distinct phases to help you achieve this.

Personal vs external

When you face a problem, you have a choice whether you view it as an external or a personal problem.

If you immediately start to turn the focus inwards and blame yourself for the problem ("How could I be so stupid?"), this is making it personal. On the other hand, if you choose to view it as a particular set of circumstances outside your influence, this is classed as external.

What percentage of life's problems do you think are exclusively down to you? Your answer will give you a good indicator of whether you are personal or external in your thinking. I reckon that about 30 per cent of our problems are completely down to us, about 40 per cent are a mixture of personal and external causes and the rest is outside our control and absolutely nothing to do with us. However, someone suffering from depression would be likely to blame 100 per cent of their problems on their own inability to do anything right. Although we can all occasionally fall into the trap of turning blame inwards, counsellors treating depression often try to address this by offering a sense of perspective.

Read this sentence:

NEW YORK
IN THE
THE AUTUMN TIME

Have you done it? Read it again.

Most people read the sentence as "New York in the autumn time". In fact, if you look carefully, it actually says, "New York in *the the* autumn time".

The reason we don't tend to spot the duplication is down to perspective. This is a key reason for us tending to personalize our problems: we don't step back and grant ourselves a sense of perspective.

Therefore, your first reaction when you are faced with a problem should be to step back and gain some perspective about where the problem really lies. This isn't to suggest that you start to point the finger of blame at others and absolve yourself of any responsibility, but equally it is too easy to allow yourself to start to blame your own failings.

Now look at the second step of being an optimistic leader.

Permanent vs temporary

How often when faced with a problem do you find yourself using words like "always", "all the time" and "never" ("I never get it right . . . This always happens to me . . . Every time I try . . . ")? Stop it! When you start to use what Thomas Edison called "pig words" (because they gobble up everything in their vicinity), what you are doing is telling others (and most crucially, yourself) that the problem you have is a permanent one.

This was an issue recognized by Sir Lawrence Holt, a shipping magnate. A number of his boats were sunk by German submarines in the Second World War and he noticed a trend in terms of the language used by those sailors who survived and those who didn't. When disaster struck, the sailors who gave permanence to their language ("We'll never be saved") tended not to survive. Those who eradicated these phrases and viewed their predicament as only temporary had a higher chance of survival.

My own favourite example of viewing problems as temporary comes from a young member of the Collyhurst and Moston Youth Club. I took a number of youngsters to the swimming baths and the lifeguard asked those who could swim to get in the deep end of the pool. One young lad jumped in and immediately started to struggle. When he was helped out of the water and had recovered, the lifeguard wanted to know why he had claimed to be able to swim when it was obvious that he couldn't. "I can swim," he replied earnestly, "just not yet!"

It is important to be realistic and careful with your own language and explanations about the length or frequency of a problem. Using words like "occasionally", "recently", "lately" and "some of the time" is far better and far more empowering for you and other people. They are also often more accurate. Too many of us tend to take on the characteristics of tabloid journalists when relaying negativity to others – the more sensational the better! Hence, we tend to over-emphasize the level or frequency of a problem.

That brings us to the third and final point.

Pervasiveness vs specific

Muhammad Yunus was awarded the 2006 Nobel Peace Prize for his work as the founder of Grameen Bank, one of Bangladesh's biggest banks. He decided that the bank could do more to help ease the crippling poverty in his own country by giving small loans to some of the world's poorest people.

When he first suggested this idea, the reactions of his friends and colleagues offered a great example of how pervasiveness often creeps into our language. They were unsupportive of the proposed venture and warned him: "*They'll* never pay the money back", "*They'll* rip you off", "*They'll* only use the money for crime/drugs/ prostitution".

Pervasiveness is when vague, unclear and general terms like *they, everybody, no one, totally, completely* and *everything* are used. They can be dangerous terms because they don't require you to get into a particularly deep understanding of an issue, but instead offer lazy and broad generalizations. Be aware that you have a small muscle in your brain called the reticular activating system (RAS), which kicks into action when you start using pervasive words. Your RAS takes what you say and finds lots of examples to support your thinking. For example, when you decide to buy a new car, say a yellow Beetle, the next day all the cars you see on the roads are yellow Beetles. That is your RAS in action. Your RAS also applies this to problems. For example, if you say "My team never has any good ideas", your RAS will find lots of examples to support this too.

Great leaders tend to avoid making generalizations and attack their problems with pinpoint accuracy, which helps them to identify specific problems to tackle.

Muhammad Yunus chose to ignore his colleagues' pervasive responses and went ahead with his plans, choosing to judge each situation on its own individual merits rather than applying sweeping generalizations. The result? Of the four million loans he has made so far, over 99 per cent of them have been paid back in full and, most significantly, he has enabled some of the world's poorest people to become independent and self-sufficient.

Don't rush in with your own sweeping generalizations but apply accuracy to the issues you face to identify how to tackle them.

Finally, remember the words of Albert Einstein reflecting on his career when accepting the 1921 Nobel Peace Prize. He said, "I would rather be an optimist and a fool than a pessimist and right."

There is a famous story of two shoe salesmen who were sent from London to India in 1910 to look at the possibilities for opening new businesses.

Within a week, the first salesman sent a telegram to his bosses asking, "Why have you sent me here? Nobody wears shoes. No new market here. Returning home. Trip has been a waste of time."

On the same day, the second salesman sent a telegram reporting, "Great news. Nobody wears shoes. Amazing opportunity. Send more shoes and staff!"

Which one would you follow?

For further exercises on how you can improve your optimism, turn to page 158.

CHAPTER 8
MAKE A SPLASH!

"*Whistle while you work!*"

THE SEVEN DWARVES, *SNOW WHITE*.

Have you ever glanced at the lonely hearts adverts at the back of your local newspaper? Next time you get an opportunity, have a quick look at them (if you're in a relationship, make sure that you're alone when you do this or at least explain to your partner what you're doing!).

One common term you will find in the majority of the adverts is a request for potential partners to be in possession of a GSOH. For those of you not familiar with this dating jargon, this stands for Good Sense of Humour and it tends to be a quality most people look for in an ideal mate. Most of us don't like people who are too stuffy or serious, as they tend to put a dampener on everything, yet when was the last time you saw a request for a GSOH included in a job advert?

Did you know that, on average, a child laughs about 400 times a day? In contrast, an adult only laughs about 15 times. Did that just wipe a smile off your face? Sorry.

What happens to the other 385 laughs? Why is it that when we step into the grown-up world of work, a sense of humour becomes a rare commodity? Too often we are preoccupied with our own worries, stresses and the pressures of our lives and so the importance of fun doesn't even merit a mention, yet the relationship between leadership and fun is critical.

Research carried out at Colorado University suggests that playing is about more than having fun. It is through playing that all animals, including humans, learn to take on and master life's challenges.

If you could open up the top of your head and see how your brain works, you would see a brain of two halves: a left and right side. Although both sides look identical and work together most of the time, they have quite different ways of seeing the world. The left-hand side of your brain is the serious and analytical part. The right-hand side, however, allows you to see the bigger picture and enjoy a good laugh. When you are relaxed and playful, you start to work the right side of your brain more and this increases the likelihood of you being more creative and original.

Jokes are a good example of how the brain operates. They make us laugh because they present us with fresh, new perspectives. It may be in the way we view words:

Q. What's orange and sounds like a parrot?
A. A carrot.

Or our relationships:

I'm a bit down at the moment as my girlfriend has just left me . . . Still, my wife is a bit happier.

Other times, it might be a solution to a problem:

There is a legendary farmer in Cornwall whose livestock was upset by the motorists speeding past his property at 80 miles per hour. His solicitor told him that it would take time and money to bring his case to the attention of the council and to argue for a suitable police notice to be erected at the roadside, and even that would be ineffective. The shrewd old farmer came up with his own sign and it said: "PLEASE PROCEED WITH CARE. NUDIST CAMP CROSSING AHEAD."

Normally our brain provides us with structure and places barriers between ideas and concepts. This is essential for us to be able to exist, because it keeps us safe and allows us to be able to operate efficiently. When you have fun and are relaxed and playful, your brain starts connecting seemingly detached ideas and starts to see situations from a different perspective. This is the best state to be in when you want to begin creating the unexpected.

Exercise

Try to guess which common phrases the following word puzzles suggest:

YOU   JUST   ME

This represents the phrase "just between me and you". Now that you have the general idea, try these:

HEAD
HEELS

R|E|A|D|I|N|G

._____RANGE

In case you haven't solved them, the answers are "head over heels", "reading between the lines" and "point-blank range".

The same puzzles were used in a study to understand how play can affect performance. Volunteers were presented with these word puzzles and asked to solve them as quickly as possible. After a 15-minute break when they could relax, the same volunteers were able to improve their scores by 30 per cent. They hadn't been consciously working on the problems during their break, but this period had helped their brains to view the puzzles in a new and helpful way.

Let's just stop for a second and consider this point.

Is having a fun and relaxed atmosphere at work actually to be encouraged? Surely it sounds too good to be true? Actually, no. There are numerous examples where this very practice has worked with dramatic effects, including the book you are reading.

In the fifteenth century, books were produced by a long, slow process of hand carving wooden blocks and then inking every word onto them before pressing paper against them. Johannes Gutenberg published books in this way and had spent years attempting to discover a more efficient method of producing large numbers of books, but he had little success. He found an answer when he visited a local wine festival and noticed that the press that crushed the grapes to produce the wine could be adapted to his own challenge – and so the first printing press was born.

Have a look at the clothes you're wearing. The chances are that at least one item contains some nylon. This is down to someone having fun at work. The DuPont chemical company challenged its chemists to create a synthetic material that had the same appearance as silk. After a number of years of painstaking research and tests, the chemists were still no closer to achieving a positive result and disillusionment had begun to set in among the team.

Their leader, W H Carothers, encouraged them to have some fun instead and a competition was organized to see how far they could stretch some of the materials they had created. One team amazed everyone by being able to stretch their material across the length of the whole lab. More importantly, they noticed that when it stretched to its extremes, the material became silky in appearance. This discovery resulted in the creation of nylon.

Even in times of crisis, having fun should be encouraged as it helps release the tension. Sir Ernest Shackleton, one of the greatest adventurers of all time, knew this and used games designed to promote camaraderie, hope and fortitude when his ship *Endurance* became stuck in Antarctic ice. Competitions involving racing dogs through to organizing variety shows all helped maintain morale during the nine long, dark months they were stuck and was later cited as an important reason all 22 of his crew survived.

Julian Richer, founder of UK electrical appliance retailer Richer Sounds, insists that staff at every one of his 50 branches meet once a month to discuss performance and improvements. Nothing unusual about that, you may think. However, Richer insists that these meetings take place in a local pub, where he even provides £5 per person for "liquid refreshment". He believes that "in the very different environment of a pub, all sorts of fresh and innovative ideas to improve the business start to emerge".

Richer cites the example of Terry Lovelock to explain his reasoning. In the 1980s Lovelock was responsible for writing the advertising campaign for Heineken beer and had reached a mental block when he was only days away from his deadline. He hadn't put forward any ideas and people were beginning to doubt him, especially when he left a note saying he had headed off to Marrakech. However, while he was there he woke up in the middle of the night to write down the words "Refreshes the parts other beers cannot reach" on a scrap of paper. It was to become one of the most successful adverts of all time.

Having a good laugh can even improve your memory. In one experiment where studies were carried out to prove this assertion, psychologists asked volunteers to read two newspaper articles, one a sad story and the other a funny article written by the comedian Woody Allen. At the same time, they used a novel technique to make people feel happy and sad. Half of the group were asked to hold a pencil between their teeth without it touching their lips (go on, try it!). Automatically, your face is forced into a smile. The other half of the group were asked to put a pencil in their mouth and support it using only their lips (try that one too). This forces the face into a frown. The purpose of these tasks is to make an obvious point that when people smile or frown they immediately begin to feel happy or sad.

When both groups were asked to write down everything they remembered from the two articles, the happy group remembered lots of details about both articles. The sad group tended only to recall details about the sad article. The mood they had adopted had a huge impact on their memory. Relate this back to your own workplace. When people are unhappy, they will focus on and remember the negative elements of the job.

One final incentive to be a leader who encourages the sound of laughter as the soundtrack to the working day is that it may even reduce sickness absences, as fun can actually improve your health. Dr Norman Cousins has written a number of books about the healing nature of laughter from his own personal experience, after being diagnosed with incurable cancer. He repeatedly watched his favourite Charlie Chaplin films and applied laughter therapy to his illness and then enjoyed a full and amazing recovery.

There is a myth that our working life isn't supposed to be fun, that good business is serious business and that laughter in a working environment is childish. As a leader you must reject this notion. Emotion, fun, enthusiasm, energy, passion, laughter – whatever you want to call it – is the lifeblood of any group. Make it your responsibility to foster and encourage an atmosphere where the sound of people enjoying themselves is a common one.

Smile

Smiling is infectious
You catch it like the flu
When someone smiled at me today
I started smiling too
I passed around the corner

And someone saw my grin
When he smiled, I realized
I'd passed it on to him.
I thought about that smile,
Then realized its worth,
A single SMILE just like mine,
Could travel round the earth.
So if you feel a smile begin,
Don't leave it undetected.
Let's start an epidemic quick
And get the world infected.

Author unknown

Turn to page 161 to read how you can take steps to introduce fun into your leadership style.

CHAPTER 9

TAKE HORSES TO WATER

> *First they came for the socialists.
> And I did not speak out because I was
> not a socialist.
> Then they came for the trade unionists.
> And I did not speak out because I was
> not a trade unionist.
> Then they came for the Jews.
> And I did not speak out because I was
> not a Jew.
> Then they came for me.
> And there was no one left to speak
> for me.*

PASTOR MARTIN NIEMÖLLER (1892–1984),
POEM IN US HOLOCAUST MUSEUM

Most human beings expect to be led

If you think about it, we learn our earliest lessons by copying the behaviour of our parents or our siblings; when we go to school, we are subjected to detailed instructions from our teachers. It is usually only when we start to reach our late teenage years that we start to be given the opportunity to begin forming our own opinions, are encouraged to start making decisions for ourselves and start to take a lead. Unfortunately, we are often given very little preparation or instructions on how to do this.

Psychologists have identified a behaviour that stems from this lifetime's conditioning, called the "bystander problem", which means that most people expect or assume that someone else will take action or take the lead. Robert Caldiani, an American psychologist, identified this after he had been fascinated by an incident that took place on a busy New York street, where 38 people had watched a young woman being attacked and not one of them had alerted the police. All 38 witnesses later stated that they had assumed that someone else had done so.

Caldiani set up a series of experiments to prove that this behaviour was a natural human condition. In one of his experiments, an actor staged an epileptic fit. When there was only one person present, 85 per cent of individuals took immediate action and helped the victim to recover.

However, when four were people present to observe the seizure taking place, these individuals all assumed that someone else would help and so assistance was only actually offered 30 per cent of the time.

This pattern of response rates was also consistently repeated in experiments where people saw smoke coming out from underneath a doorway, indicating that a fire was taking place.

In summary, it was proved that most people, when in a group, assume that someone else will take the lead. This natural reluctance to lead can create a leadership vacuum.

I will come back to this point in a moment.

Four-minute warning

Remember in the film *Jerry Maguire* when Tom Cruise visits his ex-girlfriend's house, wanting to win her back? He finds the house full of women complaining about men and so he launches into a great long speech, explaining how much he loves her. But Renée Zellwegger, who plays the object of his adoration, stops him halfway through his speech with the line: "Stop right now. You had me at hello."

A number of studies prove that this reaction is a common one for most people.

When you first come into contact with someone, studies prove that the impression you make in the first four minutes is the one that will have the greatest impact on them, no matter how much time you spend with them. In these initial four minutes we quickly judge a person and this judgement is the one that tends to stick. This principle resulted in OJ Simpson employing eight – yes, eight – stylists to advise him on his clothes and his general appearance when he appeared in court. He knew that the jurors would be making quick, snap decisions about him based on his initial appearance and that these judgements would remain the same despite the evidence presented to them.

So the first four minutes are critical.

When you are on your way into work, it is worth thinking about how you can use this time to establish yourself as a leader from the very first second you walk through the door. Remember, most people expect to be led, so if you act as a leader and make the right kind of impact during the first four minutes of the day, others will automatically see and regard you as a leader.

Don't worry if you are not an official leader or you believe that this is the responsibility of others. The point of this book is that we all have the capacity to lead and, as detailed above, there is a natural reluctance in most people to do this; don't be one of them.

Lead by example

The following words, which are written on the tomb of an Anglican Bishop in the crypts of Westminster Abbey, demonstrate the importance of leading by example.

66
When I was young and free and my imagination had no limits, I dreamed of changing the world. As I grew older and wiser, I discovered that the world would not change, so I shortened my sights somewhat and decided to change only my country. But it seemed too immovable. As I grew into my twilight years, in one last desperate attempt, I settled only for changing those closest to me but alas, they would have none of it. And now, as I lie on my deathbed, I suddenly realise: if I had only changed myself first, then by

example I would have changed my family. From their inspiration and encouragement, I would have then been able to better my country and who knows, I may even have changed the world. 🗝

The behaviours you demonstrate when you begin taking the lead will spread like a virus among those who view you as the leader. So if you are enthusiastic and optimistic, others will subconsciously follow suit. It is important that you take Gandhi's advice and "be the change that you want to see".

Why not aim to start your own equivalent of the 100 Monkey Syndrome? Let me explain further.

A tribe of monkeys based on an island near Japan were only used to eating food that they could easily take from the trees and eat immediately. Therefore, biologists buried sweet potatoes on the island, to see how the monkeys would react to this change.

Initially the monkeys wouldn't even touch the potatoes, because they were covered in sand and dirt, until eventually one young monkey took the lead and tried washing a potato in a stream before he tasted it. He discovered that he actually enjoyed this new kind of food.

This one monkey taught his mother and his friends to try the same thing, and they also discovered that they liked the sweet potatoes. They in turn taught their friends, who taught their friends and so on. After the new behaviour was adopted by 100 monkeys, the biologists discovered that all the monkeys in the tribe followed the initial lead and eating sweet potatoes became the common way of behaving.

How many people do you need to affect until following your lead becomes a natural reaction?

The guy in the glass

When you get what you want in your struggle for pelf,
And the world makes you King for a day,
Then go to a mirror and look at yourself,
And see what that guy has to say.

For it isn't your Father, or Mother, or Wife,
Who judgement upon you must pass.
The feller whose verdict counts most in your life
Is the guy staring back from the glass.

He's the feller to please, never mind all the rest,
For he's with you clear up to the end,
And you've passed your most dangerous, difficult test
If the guy in the glass is your friend.

You may be like Jack Horner and "chisel" a plum,
And think you're a wonderful guy,
But the man in the glass says you're only a bum
If you can't look him straight in the eye.

You can fool the whole world down the pathway of years,
And get pats on the back as you pass,
But your final reward will be heartaches and tears
If you've cheated the guy in the glass.

Dale Wimbrow (1895–1954)

Turn to page 161 for further exercises relating to this chapter.

Liquid Leaders

Kevin Sinfield

Kevin Sinfield joined the Leeds Rhinos rugby league team in 1996 and made his debut when he was 16 years old. He was appointed as club captain in 2003 and became the first Leeds captain ever to lift the World Club Challenge trophy and to lead his side to victory in the Powergen Challenge Cup and Grand Final. He also plays for England and for the Great Britain side.

I learned an important lesson about leadership at a young age. I had joined Leeds as a 13-year-old schoolboy and had signed as a professional immediately after reaching 16. The day after my GCSE exam results had come out and all of my friends were nursing hangovers after spending the night celebrating, I was sitting at home feeling a mixture of excitement and terror as I prepared to make my debut for the first team, as the youngest-ever forward to play Super League Rugby, against Sheffield.

As I sat at home, I thought about how my team mates, the Leeds fans, the opposition and the media would all respond to me, as it was the first time I had ever played against adults. It then occurred to me that there was no point in spending time and energy worrying about these issues, as I had no control over them. Instead, I forced myself to focus on the things I could control, such as my own performance, and this was a great help in making my debut a memorable day. I have since tried to remember this lesson throughout my whole career: looking after the things I can control and not worrying about the rest.

Another critical leadership lesson, which has helped mould me into the person I am today, came just a few years after my debut. I had begun to establish myself as a first-team player at Leeds and had played in every game during our successful cup run, which culminated in us reaching the Challenge Cup Final, which was played in Edinburgh's impressive Murrayfield Stadium. Just three days before the final, I was devastated to be told by the coach that I would not be selected to play in the final because of my lack of experience. I am not ashamed to admit that I was completely crushed by the news, not least because I felt responsible for letting down my family and friends, who had all planned to travel to Scotland and support me. More importantly, however, I felt that the reason given for my de-selection was not entirely true and I did not appreciate being treated with a lack of honesty.

After I had been through the mixed emotions of watching my team mates suffer a narrow defeat, I went back to the quiet of my hotel room and I resolved to remember this experience as a motivation to achieve my own goals. Despite feeling at a low ebb, I sat down and wrote down a list of the goals and targets that I wanted to achieve in my career, including regaining my place in the team and playing in the World Cup. I also decided that when I was in a position of leadership, trust and honesty would be the most important qualities I would display to others.

A few years later, the team endured a period of transition, which included the appointment of a new coach and the selection of a number of younger players into the first team. I was approached by the coach and asked if I would consider assuming the responsibility of captaining the team. Before I accepted, my first thought was about the deposed captain. My own experience from the cup final was still fresh and before I made a decision, I spoke with him to ensure that he had been made aware, as I wanted to ensure that he was treated with honesty and respect.

I was honoured to accept the leadership role as I had done the job before in junior teams, but I was aware that I was just 22 and there were a number of other players in our dressing room who were more senior in both years and experience. I was confident that they would recognize the importance of the team rather than any individual, and so I didn't try to take the lead by assuming that my position carried automatic authority. I was eager to use the skills and experience of all team members and so I would frequently be honest with them and ask for advice, opinions and judgements. I would even get others to deliver key team messages to make sure that repeatedly hearing my voice didn't become boring for the players. The best teams I have ever been involved with have always had a collection of leaders and I have always tried to foster the same approach.

Once I had taken over as the captain, I continued to focus on a number of small things that helped to emphasize my role as the team's leader. I would be the first player out on the field for training and I would work even harder on improving my own game. I also encouraged others to focus on the controllable elements of their own game rather than allowing any distractions to concern them. I soon saw that these good habits started to breed among the players and became a natural way of working.

Towards the end of my first year as captain we reached the Challenge Cup Final, where we met the Bradford Bulls, who were the favourites to win the game. We refused to concede anything and it was an incredibly tight game. With just three minutes remaining, we were trailing by two points when we were awarded a penalty. As the leader, I had to make a quick decision. I could either choose to take the kick, which would have drawn us level, or we could go for a try, which if it succeeded would win us the cup. I looked at the body language of both teams and I felt that we had our opponents mentally and physically beaten. Instead of taking the safe option of settling for a draw, I decided that we would dare to win and go for the try.

Unfortunately, my decision didn't pay off and we made an elementary mistake that meant we lost the final by two points. The reaction of the press and the fans was to blame me for making the decision that cost us the final and it was important that I took responsibility for my actions and was able to explain them. Daring to win rather than playing it safe or attempting to avoid defeat is an important decision that every team has to make at some stage. It was important that we learned from it; it hadn't paid off for us on this occasion, but by experiencing the hostile reaction to our defeat, it would make us less afraid of failure in the future.

The following season saw the team reach the Grand Final, which is the most difficult trophy to win as it is the result of a long, sustained season's performance. Leeds hadn't won the trophy for over 32 years and had acquired a reputation of being the "nearly men" of the game. It was anticipated by many that we would retain our tag of being unlucky losers after meeting the Bradford Bulls once again. It was important that many of the important leadership lessons I had learned during my career were implemented in the build-up to the game.

The high-profile nature of cup finals ensures that there are a lot of distractions in the build-up to the game. The lesson I learned before my debut – completely focusing on the things within your control rather than worrying about the history or the occasion – proved helpful. Secondly, the experience of the previous year's final meant that we approached the game without any fear of defeat. We had experienced the disappointment and knew that we could cope with it, so our attitude of daring to go out and win was increasingly hardened.

Finally, I was able to draw on my own experiences in being able to handle players who were disappointed not to be involved in the final game. I could understand how they felt and it was important to speak to them honestly and explain the importance of everyone in the squad remaining completely aligned and together in our quest for victory.

The final was another closely fought game, but the siege mentality we had developed in our camp was a great help in ensuring that we were successful in ending the trophy drought. At the end of the game, it is a tradition for the winning captain to give a speech in front of 75,000 fans at Old Trafford. When I was handed the microphone it was the first time I allowed myself to stop and take it all in. I was able to think of my family and friends in the stands, who had been so supportive of me throughout my career. It was also the first time my son Jack had come to a game. His birth, only a few months earlier, had helped me retain a sense of perspective throughout all of the pressures of the final. When all of the players climbed into the stands to celebrate with loved ones, it was a very special moment.

This success has acted as another catalyst for me. My ambitions for the team are now greater than ever. The hallmark of all great teams is to achieve sustained success and I want to help lead Leeds to many more trophies. I also want to continue to improve as a player and a captain and to be seen as a good example to others. I will only achieve this through my actions rather than my words. When I finish my playing career, I am determined that my team mates will remember me as an honest captain. This, along with the resulting trust and belief, are the most important characteristics for any leader.

CHAPTER 10
DEEP DIVE

> *I shall always be a flower girl to Professor Higgins because he treats me as a flower girl and he always will.*

ELIZA DOOLITTLE, *MY FAIR LADY*

In the musical *My Fair Lady*, Professor Higgins, a wealthy academic, wins a bet with his friend, Colonel Pickering, that he can take an ordinary Cockney flower girl and pass her off as a duchess among London's high society merely by refining her speech and dress. After he finally succeeds, the flower girl, Eliza Doolittle, suggests that the only real difference between a lady and a humble flower girl is "not how she behaves but how she is treated". These nine words are critical for all leaders.

Let me explain further.

In the 1950s, psychologists carried out a famous experiment in schools to test whether the expectations of the teachers had an impact on their pupils' success. They told the staff that certain children had been identified as being late bloomers and were certain to do well in the future. In reality, however, all of these children had been picked completely at random and were no different to the rest of the class.

Without consciously realizing it, over the next few months the teachers began to give these specially identified children more encouragement and praise and allowed them to ask extra questions in the classroom. Incredibly, all these so-called late bloomers then went on to achieve better test scores than the other children in the same class.

What had happened, quite simply, was that by increasing their expectations of the children's abilities, the teachers had started to encourage the children to behave in a way that transformed their expectations into a reality. Eliza Doolittle's claim was proven correct.

It is a valuable exercise to look closely at your own expectations of people. Do you expect them to be honest, trustworthy and self-motivated, or do you not trust them as far as you can throw them? The answers to these questions are integral to the results you get.

Another study, intended to support the classroom experiment, highlighted the importance of trust. A group of children were given the freedom to choose their food for a whole month. Initially, most parents expected the children to choose the food they were not usually allowed, such as chocolates and sweets. Although this was the case in the first few days, the children's own common sense soon took over and when the first giddy thrill of freedom had passed, all the children chose to eat a healthy and balanced diet.

One company that has high expectations of its employees is the takeaway sandwich chain Pret A Manger. The company's leaders believe that getting the right staff is absolutely essential to its success. Therefore job applicants are invited to work in one of the stores for a day and at the end of that day the staff take a vote, based on clear criteria, on whether the applicant is the sort of person they – and the customers – want to deal with on a regular basis. Only one in ten applicants gets appointed, but the company's leader, Andrew Rolfe, argues that this is a good thing. "We trust our people with our customers and so surely we can trust them to make the right decision about who to hire."

Would you trust your own team to make this decision for you?

A leader's expectations have the power to become self-fulfilling. For example, think about how you handle mistakes. W Edwards Demming, the man responsible for Japan's post-war industrial revival, recalled how an American company that had started to deal with a Japanese supplier issued them with a book of

requirements, which demanded that the Japanese products should conform with their own high quality standards – setting a service level of 99 per cent conformity.

Confused but happy to comply, the Japanese firm
deliberately shipped one faulty component with every
box containing 999 perfect ones. It attached a note stating
that it was unsure why the customer wanted a 0.1 per cent
failure rate, but was happy to oblige. It was treated as if it
would make mistakes and so it behaved accordingly.

Andrew Carnegie, who was once the world's richest man,
felt compelled to consider his own expectations and attitudes towards others when he began a career as a foreman,
helping to build the railways of America. After analysing
the amount of work his team got through in a day, he soon
spotted a pattern emerging. In the mornings his men would
lay nearly twice as much track as they managed in the
afternoon. Initially, he tried to improve the situation by
using a number of combinations of shift patterns, until
eventually one of his own men suggested that they should
enjoy more regular breaks and a shorter day.

What would your initial reaction be to this suggestion?

Carnegie said that his own instinct told him that the men
could be trusted, and so he agreed to adopt this new working
pattern – and discovered that his team actually increased
their productivity by 50 per cent. He later claimed that this
example caused him to regularly challenge his own expectations and was one of the most important lessons he learned
and practised on his meteoric rise to success.

Time and time again, studies have proven that a
leader's expectations can have a profound impact on
the effectiveness of their teams. Your expectations have

the power to become self-fulfilling prophecies, so why set them at a low level?

Sir Richard Branson sums this up best by suggesting, "You should never set out expecting that people will do wrong. Expect people to perform at their best and they will frequently deliver it."

Once upon a time, many years ago, two travellers were riding on a ferry across a great river that flows between two distant lands. As much to pass the time as anything, the first traveller decided to strike up a conversation with the ferryman.

"What are the people like on the far side of the river?"
The ferryman looked at him curiously. "What are the people like where you have come from?"

The traveller grunted in disgust. "Horrible, selfish, greedy and mean spirited. That's why I'm leaving!"

The ferryman shook his head sadly. "I'm afraid you'll find the people on this side of the river just the same."

A bit later in the journey, a second traveller approached the ferryman and once again asked, "What are the people like on the far side of the river?"

The ferryman looked at her curiously and asked her, "What are the people like where you come from?"

The traveller sighed. "Wonderful, kind, supportive and generous. I'm sorry to leave them behind," she said.

The ferryman smiled. "I wouldn't worry about it. I think you'll find the people on this side of the river are much the same."

Turn to page 164 for exercises relating to this chapter.

CHAPTER 11

FLUIDITY

" Creativity distinguishes between a leader and a follower. "

STEVE JOBS

By nature, all human beings are inquisitive animals. Research has repeatedly shown that when we are faced with a choice between the tried and tested and the untried and unproven, we're still more likely to choose the latter. This rule also applies when we choose our leaders. We are often more inclined to follow a leader who is stimulating, intriguing and sometimes unorthodox than a leader who comes across as conventional and plain vanilla.

There are, of course, limits to the amount of stimulation and intrigue we will tolerate, but when a leader is able to inspire others to tackle new kinds of challenges, consider alternative approaches and embrace brand new ideas, people will, to quote Colin Powell about one of his own early army mentors, "follow them anywhere, if only out of a sense of curiosity".

But being a creative leader is easier said than done. We all tend to follow routines in our lives, both at work and at home, and we quickly become comfortable dealing with these familiar patterns. We do this in order to cope with the constant demands life places on us. However, there exists a real danger that without a regular injection of creativity, we can quickly find ourselves like the fabled frog who, when placed in a pan of boiling water, jumps straight out, but when it's placed in warm water, which is slowly heated, becomes unaware of the temperature changing before being boiled to death.

It is easy to get into too much of a routine and fail to spot the changes that take place around us. You don't believe me?

Try this simple test and complete the sequence:

I, II, III, ___, V, VI, VII, VIII, IX, X

I'll bet the number you wrote is IV. Am I correct? 90 per cent of people who complete the test also assume that is the answer. But it's wrong.

The correct numeral is IIII. This is the Roman numeral system that is used on all traditional clock faces (including Big Ben, the world's most famous clock face) and that you probably see dozens of times a day. So why did you fail to recognize it and write down the numeral you may be more familiar with? The truth is that you're conditioned to respond to patterns and routines far more than you may think.

Still don't believe me? Let me give you another example. Have you ever thought why the letters on a computer keyboard are arranged in the order they are, known as the QWERTY system? Most people assume that the reason is something to do with efficiency and ease of typing.

Wrong!

The QWERTY method is probably the most inefficient system you could ever create. It was designed to slow down typists, because typing too quickly would cause the keys of a typewriter to stick. Additionally, it wasn't designed with typists in mind. Have a look at the top line of a computer: the letters that spell the word TYPE-WRITER are all contained here. The QWERTY method helped salesmen make it look easy to type rather than help users type at speed.

The reason I offer these examples is to demonstrate that you can easily get into a rut in your thinking, assuming that the normal approach is the best one and failing to spot ways to improve. Lance Armstrong, the seven-times Tour de France winner, believes that "the only difference between a rut and a grave is the size of the hole you are in".

Recognizing that you are in a rut is important for a creative leader. Don't do what you did yesterday just because you did it yesterday. Keep challenging yourself to think creatively, act creatively and be creative. Bill Gates believes that "companies that don't embrace creativity don't survive and leaders who don't embrace creativity should be replaced".

Let's look at some methods you can use to do this.

Suspend your immediate judgement

When looking for new ideas, the traditional approach is to hold a brainstorming session. Without having any mental warm-up, people tend to plough straight into the session and after suffering an initial awkward silence, one or two ideas are tossed in. These tend to be greeted by a plethora of judgemental responses about why they won't work and then, rather than get into a free-wheeling creative debate, you end up getting dragged into a mundane discussion about practicalities. The need for creativity quickly gets lost.

Suspending your judgement does work.

Humphrey Walters used this approach when he helped the England coach, Sir Clive Woodward, plan to win the 2003 Rugby World Cup. They created a climate where there were "no stupid ideas" and encouraged the players to make suggestions to improve the team. One example of the efficiency of this approach came when they discussed redesigning the changing rooms. Faced with a low budget, one of the players suggested inviting the TV programme *Changing Rooms* to carry out the work instead. Walters suggested that if the "no stupid ideas" rule had not been in effect, this idea would merely have been laughed at and ignored. Instead, it was given proper consideration and was enthusiastically taken up with great success.

Some companies have developed their own systems to deal with the typical but unhelpful approach of rushing straight into offering a critical judgement on new ideas. Southwest Airlines has creativity meetings where "undermining, critical or judgemental comments" (they call these comments "zingers") are banned. If anyone uses a zinger in response to a new idea, they have to pay a penalty.

Jimi Hendrix was praised for using a similar approach in his desire to become a legendary rock guitarist. His manager claims that he once spent a whole night in a club listening to a guitar player who was charitably referred to as "the worst guitar player in the history of the planet Earth". When his manager asked him why he wanted to stay to listen to the noise, Hendrix refused to rush in and judge but said, "So far, this is bad, but he might just play something that has never been played before. If he does – I want to be here to learn from it."

Look to understand

Next, seek to gain a better understanding of the new ideas being offered. Take the advice of another rock legend, Johnny Nash, and start looking for more questions than answers.

There is little point in creating a climate where people can freely contribute ideas without being judged if you don't then try to gain a greater understanding of the ideas. Don't be afraid to ask for more information and find out why the owner of an idea is so excited about it by asking where it comes from. There is likely to be a rich stream of creativity underpinning the answers you get.

The comedian Peter Kay recounted that he liked reading obituaries in the newspaper and once asked his mother how all those people had managed to die in alphabetical order! Joking aside, one way you may want to get a greater understanding is by asking similarly playful questions.

When an idea is offered, simply asking questions such as "Why?" and "How?" begins to make the idea broader. You should only stop asking these questions when you feel you understand what the real opportunity is. For example, a friend of mine who ran his own business shared his challenge of getting better people to come and join his team. By asking him "Why?" enough times, we discovered that he wanted to be able to confidently delegate responsibility to others and spend more time at home with his kids. This was the real issue for him and so by starting to ask how he could make this happen, we came to a number of creative solutions such as bringing his family to work, spending a day a week working from home, introducing family-friendly policies and even increasing his prices to allow him to refuse work and free up more time!

Failing to take time to understand an idea almost cost 3M one of its greatest successes: the humble Post-it note. Employee Arthur Fry was so fed up with the page marker that kept falling out of his church hymn book, he developed a marker backed with "failed" experimental glue, which had been rejected because of its low sticking power. When he presented his marker idea to the bosses, they rejected it. They omitted to ask why it had been created or how it could be used and didn't grasp its use or relevance. Fortunately for them, Fry made some prototypes and gave them to secretaries in the business, who found them indispensable. The bosses noticed and only then developed their understanding of the concept.

As a leader it is your duty to assume that every idea may be a potentially sticky one.

Try to build

Finally, once an idea has passed through the first two stages, it is important that you try to do something with it. One way of doing this is to build on the idea or make it even better.

This is what Baron Marcel Bich did when he was given an early prototype of the ballpoint pen, which was regarded as an expensive luxury item because it was used exclusively by Second World War fighter pilots. Bich used his own knowledge of plastic moulding to build on the idea of the pen and began to produce cheap plastic versions of it, which he called Bic pens. He didn't stop there, as he then used the same concept to create the disposable lighter and the plastic razor.

You too should look to find alternative uses for an idea or a particular angle that it could be used for.

This reminds me of one of my favourite stories of creativity at work. In Idaho, the government passed a law that banned nudity in public. The impact on the local strip clubs was catastrophic. One club owner refused to stop looking for a way round the problem. He finally decided to build on the law rather than fight it and challenged whether nudity was allowed if it was for "serious artistic merit". On this basis nudity was allowed, and so he began issuing all of his customers with a sketchpad and pencil to ensure that his business continued to boom.

Don't get caught unawares when a great idea comes your way, but look to build, diversify, refine and adapt it for a specific purpose.

One way to begin to inject some creativity today is by thinking about your job title and what it actually means.

Psychologists conducted an ingenious experiment to prove the importance of a job title. Two groups of participants sat in front of a computer screen and were asked to press a button whenever a light came on the screen. The first group were simply told to react as quickly as possible. Meanwhile, the second group were told to imagine themselves as daring fighter pilots who possessed razor-sharp reactions.

Amazingly, every time this test has been carried out, the people in the second group respond with far quicker reaction times. The critical factor is how they see themselves.

The Australian cricket team, who are generally regarded as the best in the world, adopt a similar strategy when they prepare to play. When they take the field against batsmen, they are asked to imagine themselves as a pack of hungry, scavenging hyenas surrounding a wounded wildebeest. This encourages them to be alert and ready for opportunities to strike against their opponents.

So how would you describe yourself and your team? Are you like lean, hungry lions hunting your prey or a group of plodding elephants sauntering along?

I remember once working in a factory where the men who were responsible for putting the tops onto bottles were commonly known as the "cap twatters". Despite the insulting title, they loved it as it gave them a sense of identity.

Why not play around with your own job title and change it to fit with your expectations of the job? One French pharmaceutical company recognizes the importance of the leaders to its own operation and refers to them by the job title *porter de sens*, which literally means "carrier of meaning". They are the people who define what the company stands for.

Martin Luther King once suggested, "If a man is called a street sweeper, he should sweep streets even as Michelangelo painted or Beethoven composed music, or Shakespeare wrote poetry." This is a good guide when encouraging others to review their own job titles.

Exercise

Have a look at the following job titles and see if you can guess the actual jobs they refer to:

1. I am a talent facilitator.

2. I am a dispenser of enthusiasm.

3. I am the Michelangelo of the hospitality world.

4. I'm a fireman tackling raging infernos.

5. I'm a big outflow pipe, pouring out all this stuff."

6. I'm a cancer sufferer first and a champion second.

Answers

1. What a great way to see your job as coach of the most talented footballers in the world! This is a quote from Carlos Alberto Parreira, the head coach of the Brazilian football team.

2. Dispenser of enthusiasm: isn't that a brilliant description? Are you a dispenser of enthusiasm? The man who said this was Stephen Spielberg, the world's most successful film maker.

3. This was the way Conrad Hilton, the founder of the world's biggest hotel chain, chose to see his work.

4. When a journalist asked Harrison Ford why he keeps making movies, he gave this reply. His career isn't driven by money, but by passion and excitement.

5. Who's the world's most successful living author? He's written more than 50 best-selling novels, many of which have been turned into movies. Stephen King described his job in this way.

6. This may seem a surprising inclusion, but the words are those of Lance Armstrong, seven-times winner of the Tour de France. He was given only a 40 per cent

chance of surviving cancer before he recovered to return and win his titles. He explained, "I wanted to show the world that a cancer victim could recover to become the best cyclist in the world. Cancer gave me this sense of purpose and I never forget that."

It may seem silly and a little contrived, but a name does matter. Just ask the marketeer from Nissan who decided to launch a new car for the Australian market and call it the Cedric. Not surprisingly, sales were disastrous.

The final tip on how to be a creative leader is to be creative yourself. Nolan Bushnell, founder of Atari, believes that "everyone who has ever taken a shower has had an idea. It's the person who gets out of the shower, dries off, and does something about it that makes a difference."

Liquid Leaders

Simon Clifford

Simon Clifford is a former school teacher who developed his own coaching programme teaching Brazilian football skills, which were unheard of in Europe at the time. Clifford set out to train his first batch of young footballers with his new methods with a notably different philosophy, preferring to concentrate on improving ball skills and close control instead of the traditional emphasis on fitness and physical strength. He has since expanded his Brazilian Soccer Schools coaching franchise to other regions and countries.

Clifford has also purchased the non-league football club Garforth Town and has expressed the desire to take the club into the FA Premier League within 20 years. So far the club has gained one promotion under Clifford's stewardship. However, he has managed to attract a number of high-profile footballers to play for the team, including Lee Sharpe, Sócrates and Careca.

He also owns SOCATOTS, a pre-school coaching programme, the first in the world to teach basic ball skills, movement and coordination exercises to children as young as six months old. This programme runs throughout the UK and internationally.

In 1996 I was teaching at a primary school called Corpus Christi based in a fairly tough area of Leeds called Halton Moor. I really enjoyed this period in my life and I put absolutely everything into it. I was running the school football team and I would organize them right down to the tiniest detail. We used to win everything in the Leeds area and this had a really positive effect on the school. If I'd had my way, I would have liked to keep the school open all year round, including the holidays, and schedule activities for the children, because I recognized that they would start to realize their potential by giving them some hope, attention and direction.

During this period, the local council released a whole raft of statistics relating to the Halton Moor estate – most of it was negative, particularly in relation to health. As a school, we decided to do something about this and started a health promotion week. We made sport a big part of this. I managed to persuade some of the guys from Yorkshire Cricket and from the Leeds Rhinos rugby league team to come down, so that the kids would be inspired by meeting their heroes. I had also arranged for Gary Speed, who at the time was playing football for Leeds United, to come along as well. Unfortunately, Gary was unable to make it. This set in chain a series of events that would alter the direction of my life and force me to become a leader.

I am originally from Middlesbrough and am a 'Boro fan and my dad and I were season ticket holders. During this time, the club had moved our seats to the most expensive area of the ground, which was the same area where the players' families and friends sat. Juninho, a little Brazilian star, had recently joined the club and was beginning to make a big impact. I was thrilled by this because since 1982, when the great Brazilian team played in the World Cup in Spain, Brazil had always held a fascination for me. In particular, I was amazed by the way they played the game of football in an entirely different style to what I had been used to watching.

Anyway, to cut a long story short, I had seen a picture of Juninho and his father, Oswaldo, in the newspapers and I soon realized that it was Oswaldo who sat in the seat behind me. Over a few cups of coffee, I gradually became friends with both him and later Juninho and became a guide and aide to them as they settled into living in England. Juninho was used to following a strict training regime and practised three times a day, yet Middlesbrough, which had paid a lot of money for him, now insisted that he only train once a day (and sometimes for just 45 minutes and occasionally not at all!). Juninho's own strict training regime from Brazil struck a chord with me, as I came from an athletics background and was used to training very hard and working towards long-term goals. I could see that this approach was not reflected in football and I felt that football was way, way behind other sports in terms of technical training and the development of the young athletes. I assumed, however, that the people who were working in the game knew better.

As Gary Speed couldn't come to the school, I arranged for Juninho to come instead. He was fantastic; he really got involved in all we were doing at the school and happily joined in with the team practices. After spending a day with us, Juninho asked me when the children did their Futebol de Salão. At that point I had no idea what this was, but he explained that children in Brazil are brought up first playing Futebol de Salão, with a small, heavy ball that doesn't bounce. He added that he didn't kick a normal ball until he was 15 years old.

I was instantly intrigued by this and the more and more I questioned Juninho on this game and how it was used in Brazil, the more fascinated I became. Juninho kindly arranged for some balls to be sent from Brazil to the school and as soon as we began to use them, I could immediately see that there was something special about the balls. In particular, I could see the increase in the children's confidence because they were getting more touches of the ball.

I began spending a considerable amount of time with Juninho and his father and I was constantly quizzing them on Brazilian football, on Futebol de Salão and on their training practices. It was fascinating to hear their thoughts and comparisons between football in England and Brazil. At the time, I didn't fully believe their claims that even the smallest street club in Brazil was more organized and detail conscious than even the very biggest football clubs in England. Now that I have seen this for myself I can fully understand what he meant, but at the time it was hard to believe, as I felt that surely the highly paid professionals and experts employed in UK football clubs knew best.

I wrote to various organizations, including the Football Association and the Sports Council, to see if they had any more information on Futebol de Salão or indeed whether it was something they had ever considered implementing. I didn't really get anything back, certainly nothing positive. However, I had become so convinced that this was something we needed here and I decided to go to Brazil to study how they trained. I borrowed against my teaching pension to cover the cost of the trip, and I asked Juninho to help me contact the appropriate clubs and coaches.

The trip was a real eye-opener and I managed to meet with everyone I had aimed to see. When I came back to Leeds, I was more convinced than ever that this was something I wanted to pursue. The three key things I took from my Brazilian experience were the use of Futebol de Salão in training, the heavy emphasis on technical skills and repetition, and the increased training time that young players carried out in Brazil. To emphasize this last point, 12 and 13 year olds at professional clubs in Brazil will train for around 20 hours a week, light years away from what we do here.

These were my key findings from Brazil and I was determined to implement them at the school. I soon started an out-of-school session on a Saturday morning for the kids and these sessions were the real starting point for my Brazilian Soccer Schools.

At this time I had no real plans to do anything else other than to work with the kids in this small part of Leeds and to see what could happen from there. However, there soon started to be quite a lot of media interest in what I was doing, and people began to come to Leeds to visit me and watch how I was training the children. There seemed to be a bit of magic in the air and one ITV film crew visited us and said that our training, in that little school gym in a poor area of Leeds, was the most impressive training they had ever seen. What made this feedback so valuable was that this crew were filming a documentary on youth football training and had consequently been all round the world, visiting the likes of Ajax, Inter Milan and Boca Juniors. This gave me great heart that my instinct had been correct.

The interest in what I was doing started to grow and I then began to contemplate whether it would be possible to make more of a difference and get my training programme up and running in other areas of the country. This was how I came up with the idea of running the Brazilian Soccer Schools as a franchise, as I certainly didn't have the money to pay people to run schools in Edinburgh, Manchester, London and elsewhere in the country. I kept the franchise very cheap to ensure that good football people with a similar attitude to me got involved, and this is how we started. I had backing from Mitre in helping to develop the Futebol de Salão ball and we began the original group of franchises with our first ever training course in July 1999.

That same year I had another key breakthrough, as I managed to persuade Lego to join me as my main sponsor, which was a huge three-year deal worth nearly £3 million. This sponsorship really allowed me to push on with all of my plans and ideas and move at an accelerated pace. Until that point we had no real structure ourselves, to the extent that when I signed the deal with Lego I didn't even have my own offices but was working upstairs in my house! I am not sure that Lego ever realized that, but its support was key. The company believed in the future vision I painted and through its help and support, I have now made great strides towards making that vision a reality.

These were the first steps I took to make my mark as a leader and established the Futebol de Salão and Brazilian Soccer Schools as the biggest and the best in the world. I now have many more strings to my bow, including the SOCATOTS business, owning and managing Garforth Town and my Lesonn charity project.

Despite this success, I am continuing to work towards the vision I had when I started out. I want to change the culture of football, including the culture of how we both play and train for the game. At the same time, I want to ensure that young people involved in my programme have the opportunity to learn the lessons and discipline that will help them get a good education as well as improving their football skills. I have made some progress, and with graduates from my schools, like Manchester City's Micah Richards making his England international debut, I are getting closer all the time, but there is still much to do.

My schools and my own example can play a part in inspiring young people to believe that they too can step forward to take the lead and achieve their own dreams and ambitions.

Are you doing the same?

CHAPTER 12
SET SAIL!

" Your time is limited, so don't let it be wasted living someone else's life. Have the courage to follow your heart and intuition. You've got to find out what you love. Do what you believe is great work. If you haven't found it, keep looking. Don't settle. "

STEVE JOBS, FOUNDER OF APPLE.

Whoever you are and whatever your circumstances and reasons for reading this book, there is one thing you already have in common with the world and history's greatest leaders: the number 1440.

No matter how rich, how poor, how famous or how capable you are, 1440 is the number of minutes you have every day of your life. Every morning you get 1440 minutes to use; every night you write off the time you have failed to invest well. Time doesn't carry over and it doesn't allow you an overdraft. If you fail to use the day's deposits, the loss is yours. There's no going back. There's no opportunity to borrow against tomorrow's amount. You must live in the present and focus on today. Invest your time wisely.

To realize the value of one year, ask a student who failed a grade.

To realize the value of one month, ask a mother who gave birth to a premature baby.

To realize the value of one week, ask the editor of a weekly paper.

To realize the value of one hour, ask the lovers who are waiting to meet.

To realize the value of one minute, ask the person who missed the train.

To realize the value of one second, ask a person who avoided an accident.

To realize the value of one millisecond, ask the person who came second in the Olympic 100 metres final.

I started this book by quoting Jerry Springer and so I will try to be a bit more highbrow by ending it by paraphrasing William Shakespeare:

" In the time of your life – lead! "

Personal postscript

Now that you've read this far, I feel I owe you some sort of explanation about how the book you are holding came into existence.

My other book, *Liquid Thinking*, focuses on how anyone can adopt simple techniques and behaviours in their lives to achieve great success. I therefore wanted this book to be about how to lead and inspire others to gain similar results.

My inspiration for this book came from a visit to the Nobel Museum in Stockholm. When I walked through the museum, I came across a section dedicated to Sir Isaac Newton that included an extract of a letter Newton had written to his friend Robert Hooke about his discoveries. He suggested, "if I have seen farther it is by standing on the shoulders of Giants." By sharing with you stories of James Timpson's trusting approach to leadership, Kevin Sinfield's honesty, Kim England's courage, Simon Clifford's creativity and Fergus Finlay's bold vision, I hope that I have been able to help you to stand on the shoulders of giants and see farther than others.

Remember the statistic that only 10 percent of books ever get read beyond Chapter 1? Well, by getting this far, you have already put yourself in a minority.

You are already a step closer to becoming a Liquid Leader.

Damian Hughes
Manchester, April 2009

Exercises

The following pages contain some ideas and exercises relating to the chapters that you can use to help you become a great leader.

Liquid assets exercise (page 22)

1. Identifying your question is one of the most important activities you can do. One exercise that can help you identify it is this:

   • Think about the three greatest achievements of your life.

   • Think about what each achievement has in common.

     Note: you should remove individual elements of each achievement. For example, if the achievement was winning a bike race the bike is an individual factor. The common factor may be your determination to win or your discipline to train.

   • There will be one factor that is evident in each achievement and this will help you identify your question.

2. Why not create a visual image of your new set of values, which you can then look at every day, like James Timpson's Mr Men?

   This will help to fill your mind with these values and help you to commit to keep working on them and behaving in a way that is consistent.

3. Sir John Harvey-Jones claimed that whenever he was unsure whether his behaviour fitted with his own values, he would ask himself the "M'lud question". He would imagine himself in a courtroom having to answer questions about his own conduct. If he didn't feel he would be prepared to justify something, he didn't do it. If you are unsure how to behave in a certain situation, ask yourself the M'lud question.

Liquid crystal display exercise (page 29)

I have helped both individuals and teams create their own visions by acting as a news reporter: interviewing people involved in the task and then focusing on what they would see, hear, feel, touch, taste and sense when the vision actually happened. This is an effective way of avoiding the creation of a vision becoming an intellectual exercise. Instead, it becomes something that is practical and relevant to everyone, especially when they can see their own words being quoted back.

Why not get someone to interview you about your vision?

Alternatively, some other ideas on how you can help craft a vision are:

- Write a two-page story about who you are (along with a scintillating plot line on how you came to be in your current situation).

- Try to boil the vision down to a poem or song that particularly captures the spirit of your vision.

This idea of having a poem as your vision was something that Muhammad Ali, the most famous sportsman in history, did when he first burst into the world's consciousness, making bold predictions about how and when he was going to win his fights. He would confidently declare his method of victory by quoting his own poems, such as:

> *"When you come to the fight,*
> *Don't block the aisles*
> *Don't lock the door,*
> *You will all be going home after round four!"*

Or:

> *"I predict that I will win in eight to prove I am great;*
> *and if he wants to go to heaven, I'll get him in seven.*
> *He'll be in a worser fix, if I cut it to six.*
> *And if he keeps talking jive, I'll end it in five.*
> *If he makes me sore; he'll go, like Archie Moore, in four.*
> *And if that don't do, I'll cut it to two.*
> *And if he runs, he'll go in one."*

He spent his whole career making similar predictions with an incredible accuracy. These predictions were the result of intense mental preparation, when he would imagine the whole fight, right up to the moment of victory, in minute detail.

In fact, his trainer, Angelo Dundee, once told me that Ali's confidence in his vision was so powerful, he would sometimes remind the photographers surrounding the ringside of his forecasts and warn them to be ready to take their pictures just before he landed the punches to end the contest.

Why not create your own poem that sums up where you are heading?

Sailing by the north star exercise (page 51)

Marketing guru Seth Godin believes that "if you can't state your position in eight words or less, you don't actually have a position" and the same is true for your life's mission.

Try to capture your position by using the following ideas:

- If you had to write a *Yellow Pages* advert for yourself, what would you say? What do you offer and why? How would it appeal to a customer? Make it no longer than half a page.

- Now, imagine writing your epitaph. What would it say to summarize your life's mission?

Drip effect exercise (page 63)

It is very important that you begin to practise how to summarize your vision, so you can repeat it regularly and help to imprint it on the minds of others.

One effective way of doing this is to imagine that you meet the world's richest man, Bill Gates, in an empty lift. When he asks what you do, it's your big opportunity to convince him to take you seriously by the time you both reach your destination. His support could prove vital in your success.

Incidentally, there is a famous story that circulates around Microsoft's offices that Gates once asked exactly that question of a nervous employee, who told him, "I work for you, Mr Gates." Gates politely corrected him with the reminder, "You don't work *for* me, you work *with* me."

Here are some tips to help you:

- In order to write the best possible elevator speech you need to generate ideas. I suggest that you start by brainstorming – either by yourself or with some-one whom you trust and who understands your vision.

- Write down all the things you do for others – in other words, how do others benefit from you, your products or services? Let your mind roam freely. Don't worry about organizing the ideas at this stage. Just jot them down as they come to you, no matter how bizarre they may be. Some of the ideas may overlap, but that's okay.

Write them all down. This is the creative process, so go with the flow.

- Next, think about the reasons people deal with you. Do you improve people's health, relationships, productivity, profits, fitness? Using another piece of paper, write down all the ideas you have in response to this question.

- Once you have stopped brainstorming, keep the lists handy so you can add to them whenever a great idea comes to you.

- Look at the ideas you have already written and choose the ones that are most likely to stimulate conversation when you meet Bill in the lift.

- You might find it helpful to break the elevator speech into two parts. The first part could describe what you do and the second part could describe the value and benefits you offer others. For example, "I help people design and landscape gardens so that they can enjoy them all year round with minimal fuss" is one speech I heard that illustrates the point.

- Next, write the speech out and practise saying it out loud. Does it get the key ideas across? Does it stimulate interest? Is it easy to say? Above all, does it sound like you?

You should also think about using other methods to communicate your vision. Break your day down into stages, such as the start of meetings, morning roll calls, lunchtimes.

Is there an obvious way of reminding people about your vision that is similar to Stelios's morning meeting or Bill Sweetenham's breakfasts?

Water gauge exercise (page 69)

Motivating yourself to persevere in the face of failure is sometimes difficult. A cost–benefit analysis is a good exercise to do whenever you feel like giving up.

First, write down your goal. Draw a vertical line down the centre of the page and write the heading "benefits" at the top of one column and "costs" at the top of the other.

Now think about how you might achieve your goal. Imagine yourself being successful and attaining whatever it is you really want to happen. As if by magic, your dream has become a reality. In the "benefits" column write down all the benefits that would flow from you achieving your goal. Think of everything you can: how achieving it might make you feel better and enrich your personal and professional life; how it might improve your income, add meaning to your life or help the people you care about most. Keep on adding to the list as you think through the various ways in which you would benefit from achieving your goal.

Next, in the "costs" column jot down some of the things that will require some effort to achieve your goal. Perhaps you will have to write a few more letters, faxes and emails, or make a few more telephone calls. Perhaps you might have to attend a few more meetings. Perhaps you will have to change a few of your habits.

Now take a step back and look at the two lists. Once again, imagine yourself achieving your goal and compare the costs associated with the benefits. When most people complete this exercise they realize that the benefits far outweigh the costs and they find themselves thinking that it is time for action.

Goal:

Benefits	Costs

Another effective exercise is the following:

- Identify one behaviour that you want to see.

- Identify all blockers to it that currently exist.

- Identify incentives that you could put in place to encourage others or yourself.

Example: Want to encourage others to be creative

Behaviour	Blocker	Incentive
Encourage creativity	Leaders are too busy to chat and pursue ideas	Suggestion box where ideas can submitted
	No evidence of any new ideas ever being adopted	Monthly meetings where time is scheduled for new ideas
	History of criticizing mistakes when creativity has gone wrong	Dedicate a space where mistakes are celebrated and can be learned from rather than punished
	Peer pressure to conform	Introduce a reward scheme for good and new ideas
	Lack of trust in team that ideas will be stolen	

Behaviour	Blocker	Incentive

(*Continued*)

Behaviour	Blocker	Incentive

Liquid sunshine exercise (page 83)

You can train yourself to be optimistic by completing a thinking record.

Be on the lookout for situations in which you have negative emotions, for example where you feel angry, frustrated, nervous, ashamed, disappointed, scared, embarrassed, lonely, hopeless, guilty. Complete the following details for each situation:

- Make a note of the emotion because this will lead you to have a negative thought ("I am stupid"). At this stage it is important that you don't let this go; this is how it builds up to become a bigger problem over time.

- Catch the thought and subject it to some analysis. Is it true? If not, what is the alternative?

Before he became a successful football manager, José Mourinho was a sports teacher and coached disabled children in football skills. He completed a chart similar to this and believes that learning to curb his own negative thinking and become an optimist is one of his greatest achievements.

Time and Date	Place	Negative emotion	Automatic negative thought	Rational alternative thought

Reading the papers on a Sunday morning is one of my greatest pleasures and I always like to predict the subsequent results of sports teams by reading the quotes of their managers. It is amazing how many of the optimistic managers achieve success compared to their negative contemporaries.

Read the following statements made by English football Premier League managers during one particular season and decide whether they are essentially optimistic or pessimistic. Try to identify which two managers achieved success at the end of the season, which one was relegated and which one was later dismissed.

1. "History tells us that we aren't mature, that we don't have the mental strength; that we aren't tough enough to come up week after week as the good teams do."

2. "There was one 20-minute spell when they were a little bit quicker to the ball than we were. I was proud of my team; however, we are a little depleted at the moment but if we keep up the same levels of passion and intensity, we will be successful."

3. "Gutless, heartless, clueless and no passion. Where do I start after a display like that?"

4. "Their passing was better than ours during the first half and our concentration levels dipped slightly. We will improve these aspects of our game and will be better next week."

Here are the answers:

1. Manager was dismissed.

2. Manager was successful in taking his team to the European Cup Final.

3. Manager's team was relegated.

4. Manager's team became the League champions.

Finally, simple affirmations can have a hugely beneficial effect on the way we think and feel. Émile Coué, a French pharmacist and psychotherapist, was one day asked for a specific medication by a very insistent patient who didn't actually have a prescription. Knowing he couldn't dispense the medicine, Coué gave him a sugar pill instead, telling him that it was an even better remedy than the one he had been asking for.

Some days later, the man, who had made a full recovery, returned to offer his thanks. Realizing that it could only have been the patient's own attitude that cured him, Coué set about creating a method to help other people benefit from the power of positive affirmations. He devised his well-known formula for those recovering from illness: that they should say aloud, 20 times every day, "Every day in every way I'm getting better and better".

Do you have a similar affirmation that you repeat during times when you feel at your lowest?

Invent your own below:

_____

Make a splash exercise (page 93)

One exercise any leader can use when struggling with a problem is to offer perspective and write the problem down before then asking the following questions:

- What's the worst that can happen?

- How can I find this funny?

- How can I turn this situation into a chance to learn something about me?

If this doesn't work, relax and walk away from the problem before approaching it again with a playful and open mind.

Take horses to water exercise (page 103)

Leading by example is a behaviour that has long been acknowledged as common to all great leaders. There is a famous story about a young foot soldier who approached Alexander the Great during a forced march across the desert with his army. Water was running desperately short and the soldier offered Alexander some of the precious liquid from his own rations. Alexander paused and then asked the soldier if he had enough water for all 10,000 men. On being told no, he slowly poured the water he'd been offered into the sand.

Within two hours, historians claimed that every single soldier knew about this incident. Huddled around their fires in the cold desert night, there was only one topic of conversation. It was accepted that they were on a horrible mission and that lives would be lost, but they were all in it together and they had the right man leading them.

Sir Clive Woodward recognized this approach when he was in charge of the England rugby team and adopted it in his half-time team talks. He called it Second Half Thinking and he used the ten minutes to influence the thinking of his players. Rather than worrying about whether they were winning or losing after the first half, he insisted on his players changing their shirts and wearing a new kit while he thought about his own words to influence the mindsets of the players and re-focus them on winning. He describes how those crucial ten minutes should be used:

0000–0002 minutes
Absolute silence
Think about performance
Shirts off
Towel down

> *New kit*
> *0–0 on scoreboard*
> **0002–0005 minutes**
> *Coach's assessment*
> *Take on food and fluids*
> **0005–0008 minutes**
> *Coach's final word*
> **0008–0010 minutes**
> *Absolute silence*
> *0–0 on scoreboard*
> *Visualize kick-off*

Why not do a similar breakdown for the first few minutes of your own day, and focus on the behaviours you want to lead by example with and demonstrate to others?

0000–0002 minutes

Behaviour:

0002–0003 minutes

Behaviour:

0003–0004 minutes

Behaviour:

Deep dive exercise (page 117)

We all have voices in our heads that are giving us information. We rarely get the opportunity to stop and listen to these voices and determine if they are giving us helpful information or not.

The "In the dock" process helps you to find out what is true and what is false in your beliefs about people. It is a great technique to discover what tricks your mind may be playing on you. It runs as follows:

- Write down your belief as a statement of fact (e.g. "I believe that people are lazy").

- Get frustrated, negative and miserable and now, with no censoring, write down everything that supports your belief. Don't analyse or restrict yourself, just scribble wildly (e.g. "most people don't like work", "most people do as little as possible to get by").

- Balance things up a bit. Be loving and nurturing and see the best in people and be as optimistic as possible (e.g. "people want to help others").

- Now read through each statement and ask whether it is true, false or don't know.

  True is something that is provable. It should stand up in a court of law. There is no judgement involved, it is the truth. False is the stuff you know deep down is rubbish. Watch out here because your brain is tricky and will often phrase things in a nebulous way that sounds true. Be strict – if it is not absolutely true, it can only be classed as false or don't know.

Sometimes you will find statements that could be true but you are not absolutely certain. If it is a prediction – for instance "my team will be less successful" – it can at best be a "don't know" because you don't know the future. However, "everyone in my team will hate me" is false because there is no way it can be true. If in doubt, write the statement again using language that is definitely true.

- By writing what is true and false your issue will change, sometimes quite dramatically. With this new perception, write down what your belief is now.

Here is an example that I used with one leader:

Belief: *My team will never be able to deliver a great presentation to the bosses*

Negative	Positive
They haven't prepared enough – FALSE	They want to do well – TRUE
They want it to go wrong – FALSE	They know this stuff better than anyone – TRUE
They are not good enough – FALSE	This is a great opportunity for them to show what they can do – TRUE

(Continued)

165

Negative	Positive
They will go blank and forget everything – DON'T KNOW	They can learn from this and get even better – TRUE
They are out of their depth – FALSE	

In this case the only DON'T KNOW is whether they will go blank, so he helped them prepare by suggesting prompt cards as a reminder. He then felt very differently about this presentation.

Recommended reading

***Born to Win: A Lifelong Struggle to Capture the America's Cup*, John Bertrand (Bantam, 1986)**
The quote at the start of this book sums up the remarkable story of how underdog John Bertrand won yachting's America's Cup: "Heroes remind us of our dreams and of our destinies. In their thousand ways, they remind us who we are." This book does just that.

***Unleash your Creativity: Fresh Ideas for Having Fresh Ideas*, Rob Bevan and Tim Wright (Perigee Books, 2007)**
An excellent book on creativity that contains lots of useful tips and advice.

***Gung Ho! Turn on the People in Any Organization*, Ken Blanchard and Sheldon Bowles (HarperCollins Business, 1998)**
Another book by the author of the *One Minute Manager* series that explains how three core ideas are enough to motivate a whole organization.

***Whale Done! The Power of Positive Relationships*, Ken Blanchard, Thad Lacinak and Jim Ballard (Nicholas Brealey Publishing, 2003)**
A brilliant little book that takes lessons from the trainers of killer whales in US theme parks and relates them to our own lives as leaders.

***Virtuoso Teams: The Extraordinary Story of Extraordinary Teams*, Andy Boynton and Bill Fischer (Financial Times/Prentice Hall, 2008)**

This book is a fascinating study of some of history's greatest ever teams, including the team who wrote *West Side Story*, Miles Davis' jazz colleagues and Thomas Edison's "muckers".

Losing My Virginity: The Autobiography, Sir Richard Branson (Virgin Books, 2007)

A fascinating insight into how a shy, dyslexic school dropout used his strengths to create a company that, in his own words, "is the only worldwide brand Britain has created in the last 60 years". It is an inspiring read.

The Game Plan: Your Guide to Mental Toughness at Work, Steve Bull (Capstone, 2006)

Bull is the sports psychologist to the England cricket team and this book is packed full of insights, tips and exercises to achieve mental toughness in the corporate world.

Influence: The Psychology of Persuasion, Robert Cialdini (HarperBusiness, 2007)

An excellent book on the psychology of large groups.

The Success Principles: How to Get from Where You Are to Where You Want to Be, Jack Canfield (Element Books, 2005)

I like Jack Canfield, one of the creators of the *Chicken Soup for . . .* books. He has a disarming style that contains some real wisdom to stir your thinking. This book is a comprehensive guide to how to be successful and is well worth a read.

The Power of Focus: How to Hit Your Business, Personal and Financial Targets with Absolute Certainty, Jack Canfield, Mark Victor Hansen and Leslie Hewitt (Vermilion, 2001)

Does what it says on the cover. Contains some good tips on how to focus on the areas of your life in which you want success.

***How to Move Minds and Influence People: A Remarkable Way of Engaging and Persuading Others*, Iain Carruthers (Prentice Hall, 2003)**

A short book about how to weave stories into your communication style to make them more memorable.

***My Life*, Bill Clinton (Arrow Books, 2005)**

Autobiography of the charismatic former US President.

***The Change Function: Why Some Technologies Take Off and Others Crash and Burn*, Pip Coburn (A&C Black, 2007)**

A study of why some technologies fail. The premise is that a change of behaviour is essential to the success of a product and how leaders can provide that.

***The Alchemist*, Paolo Coelho (Thorsons, 1999)**

This book really stirred and moved me and made me think deeply about my own life and direction. Its enduring popularity would suggest that its impact is being felt by many others too. Read this book.

***Lance Armstrong: Tour de Force*, Daniel Coyle (HarperSport, 2006)**

This is an excellent book which should be read alongside Armstrong's own accounts. Coyle is a journalist who followed the record setting cyclist during a whole season and marvels at his leadership style and dedication to carving his name into history.

***Joe DiMaggio: The Hero's Life*, Richard Ben Cramer (Simon & Schuster, 2002)**

The definitive biography of the legendary American sports figure, which looks at his great ability to inspire others.

Golden Apples: Six Simple Steps to Success, Bill Cullen (Hodder & Stoughton, 2005)

Bill Cullen is an Irish entrepreneur and philanthropist who grew up in abject material poverty but wealthy in love, care and affection. In this fascinating book, he shares the wisdom he was lucky enough to receive over 60 years ago and explains how it drove him to great success.

Seven Secrets of Inspired Leaders: How to Achieve the Extraordinary . . . By Leaders Who Have Been There and Done It, Phil Dourado and Phil Blackburn (Capstone, 2005)

I read this book from cover to cover while sitting in a café in Tallin, Estonia and it is packed with common sense and incisive points that are guaranteed to stimulate your thoughts on leadership.

Nuts! Southwest Airlines' Crazy Recipe for Business and Personal Success, Kevin and Jackie Freiberg (Texere, 1998)

A study of Southwest Airlines' unconventional approach from two independent observers.

Leading in a Culture of Change, Michael Fullan (Jossey Bass, 2007)

This book is required reading for all head teachers and is also an excellent guide for any other leader.

How to Think Like Leonardo Da Vinci: Seven Steps to Genius Every Day, Michael Gelb (Element Books, 2004)

Looks at how we can bring genius to our everyday lives.

Dream Merchants and HowBoys: Mavericks, Nutters and the Road to Business Success, **Barry Gibbons (Capstone, 2001)**

Barry Gibbons is the former head of Burger King who helped turn the business around before he quit, concentrating instead on his speaking and writing work. He writes in a brilliantly informal and humorous way about business and leadership as well as his support of Manchester City. This book is his look at some of the leaders who have had the biggest impact on our world through their ideas and how they subsequently executed them.

Warning: May Contain Nuts!, **Barry Gibbons (Capstone, 2002)**

Another entertaining look at the world of business and more specifically about Gibbons' own experiences as a corporate leader.

This Indecision is Final: 32 Management Secrets of Albert Einstein, Billie Holliday and a Bunch of Other People Who Never Worked 9–5, **Barry Gibbons (Irwin Professional, 1996)**

Gibbons's first book after leaving Burger King. It was written in 1996 but is interesting to read his initial reflections and see how accurate (or inaccurate!) some of his predictions were.

Winning Ugly, **Brad Gilbert and Steve Jamison (Pocket Books, 2007)**

Gilbert was an average tennis player who achieved far more than his talent should have allowed. How did he achieve this? Through his own mental approach to the game that he shares in this bestselling book. Gilbert is now teaching British tennis players how to apply these techniques.

***The Tipping Point: How Little Things Can Make a Big Difference*, Malcolm Gladwell (Abacus, 2002)**
Gladwell's excellent look at how change starts and carries through large groups.

***Blink: The Power of Thinking Without Thinking*, Malcolm Gladwell (Penguin, 2006)**
A brilliant book about trusting your gut instinct, filled with practical examples of where trusting that feeling in your bones really does work.

***All Marketers are Liars: The Power of Telling Authentic Stories in a Low-Trust World*, Seth Godin (Portfolio, 2005)**
This is not particularly a book aimed at marketers but at anyone who is interested in challenging their own pre-conceptions about the advertising we are bombarded with.

***Purple Cow: Transform Your Business by Being Remarkable*, Seth Godin (Penguin, 2005)**
This book suggests that being good is no longer acceptable – being remarkable is what is now required to stand out. Godin explains how.

***The New Leaders: Transforming the Art of Leadership into the Science of Results*, Daniel Goleman, Richard Boyatzis and Annie McKee (Time Warner, 2003)**
Goleman wrote a great book called *Emotional Intelligence* and this book is a great follow-up relating to leaders.

Leadership, **Rudolph Giuliani (Time Warner, 2003)**
An autobiography and a reflection on the lessons that the mayor of New York learned during his tenure as the city's leader, especially in the aftermath of the September 11th attacks.

Pond Life: Creating the Ripple Effect in Everything You Say and Do, **Jon Hammond (Capstone, 2006)**
A book packed with simple tips and techniques on communication.

Life's a Game So Fix The Odds: How to Be More Persuasive and Influential in Your Personal and Business Life, **Philip Hesketh (Capstone, 2005)**
Hesketh writes in a personable style and explains how to be more persuasive and influential. There are some great tips for leaders.

Peerless: The Sugar Ray Robinson Story, **Brian Hughes and Damian Hughes (Damian Hughes, 2007)**
When my Dad asked me to get involved in writing the biography of possibly the greatest boxer ever, I was delighted. I loved getting under the skin of this fascinatingly complex man and understanding the courage it took to stand up and be different.

Synchronicity: The Inner Path of Leadership, **Joseph Jaworski (Berrett-Koehler, 1998)**
Jaworski is the founder of the American Leadership Forum and this book is about his own journey from high-flying lawyer to inspirational leader.

How Lance Does It: Put the Success Formula of a Champion into Everything You Do, **Brad Kearns (McGraw-Hill, 2006)**

A book that studies Lance Armstrong's mental approach and how it helped propel him to success in cycling and life in general.

Leading Change, **John Kotter (Harvard Business School Press, 1996)**

Kotter is an authority on change management and this book is a must-read for anyone interested in the topic.

The Heart of Change: Real-Life Stories of How People Change Their Organizations, **John Kotter and Dan Cohen (Harvard Business School Press, 2002)**

Real life stories of change agents.

Dare: Take Your Life On and Win, **Gary Leboff (Mobius, 2007)**

Gary Leboff is a mate of mine and this book is a real indicator of just how positive, creative and challenging this life coach/sports psychologist is. I would advise you to read this book . . . and I am not being biased!

Freakonomics: A Rogue Economist Explores the Hidden Side of Everything, **Steven Levitt and Stephen Dubner (Penguin, 2007)**

This bestselling book is based around the economic principle that any behaviour can be manipulated as long as the incentives are right. The writers apply this logic to politics, parenting and drug dealers. A really stimulating read.

Moneyball: The Art of Winning an Unfair Game, **Michael Lewis (W W Norton, 2004)**
The inspiring story of how Billy Beane, the head coach of the Oakland A's baseball team, challenged conventional thinking to achieve unprecedented success.

Fat, Forty and Fired: The Year I Lost My Job and Found My Life, **Nigel Marsh (Piatkus, 2006)**
An fun book about Nigel Marsh's decision to pack in the rat race to pursue his own dreams and ambitions.

Winning with People: Discover the People Principles that Work for You Every Time, **John C Maxwell (Thomas Nelson, 2006)**
21 chapters containing some great examples of how people have stepped forward to take the lead.

Sir Alf: A Major Reappraisal of the Life and Times of England's Greatest Football Manager, **Leo McKinstry (HarperSport, 2007)**
A fantastic biography of Sir Alf Ramsey, England's most successful manager.

Sun Tzu: The Art of War for Managers, **Gerald Michaelson (Adams Media, 2001)**
For those of you who regard leadership as war, this interesting book is an application of Sun Tzu's teachings to the modern day.

You Can Have What You Want, **Michael Neill (Hay House, 2006)**
A really fun and accessible insight into the teachings of one of the world's leading success coaches, delivered with a fair degree of humour and honesty.

Mourinho: The True Story, **Joel Neto (First Stone Publishing, 2005)**
A short book, controversial due to Mourinho's attempts to ban it. It contains some interesting insights into the football manager's enigmatic leadership style.

Coaching with NLP: How to Be a Master Coach, **Joseph O'Connor and Andrea Lages (Element Books, 2004)**
An easily accessible book that offers a great insight into the techniques of neuro-linguistic programming.

Sports Leaders and Success: 55 Top Sports Leaders and How They Achieved Greatness, **William O'Neil (McGraw Hill, 2004)**
A series of short articles about great sports leaders' approaches to success.

The Damned Utd, **David Peace (Faber and Faber, 2007)**
This book is a work of genius. It gets deep inside the mind of Brian Clough during his 44 days in charge of Leeds United and highlights the maverick nature of a footballing legend trying to change the culture of a successful organization.

Re-imagine!, **Tom Peters (Dorling Kindersley, 2006)**
An irreverent approach to the challenges that twenty-first-century businesses and leaders face from an American business guru.

The Brand You 50: Reinventing Work, **Tom Peters (Alfred Knopf, 2000)**

A small book containing lots of tips and hints about how you can lead your workplace to become a better, more exciting and enjoyable place, by legendary management writer Peters.

Success Built to Last: Creating a Life That Matters, Jerry Porras, Stewart Emery and Mark Thompson (Wharton, 2006)

Porras, co-author of the bestselling business bible *Built to Last*, contributes to this enjoyable book about personal success.

The Culture Code: An Ingenious Way to Understand Why People Around the World Buy and Live as They Do, Clotaire Rapaille (Broadway Books, 2007)

This amazing book is written by a French-born, US-based psychologist who has been in great demand for many years by businesses seeking his expertise in unlocking the code that their products really represent to people. If you are at all interested in understanding the deeper meaning of advertising, cultures and people, I cannot recommend this book highly enough.

Hope: How Triumphant Leaders Create the Future, Andrew Razeghi (Jossey Bass, 2006)

A really compelling book that argues that the ability to instil hope is a critical characteristic all leaders must possess. Razeghi looks at numerous practical examples where hope has helped to salvage some desperate situations and helps to explain how anyone can become more hopeful. I have spoken with the author on a number of occasions and can testify that he does indeed live his own lessons too.

Funky Business, Jonas Ridderstrale and Kjell Nordstrom (Financial Times/Prentice Hall, 2001)

A brilliantly subversive look at the world of business through the eyes of two Swedish professors.

The IMPACT Code: Live the Life You Deserve, Nigel Risner (Capstone, 2006)

A book by a former business leader that contains many practical tips about how you can take small steps to achieve success.

You Had Me at Hello: The New Rules for Better Networking, Nigel Risner (Forest Oak, 2003)

Nigel Risner's first book tackled the issue of how to make an immediate impact. A short but entertaining read.

Authentic Happiness: Using the New Positive Psychology to Realize Your Potential for Lasting Fulfilment, Martin Seligman (Nicholas Brealey Publishing, 2003)

Seligman is the authority on optimism. Read this book to understand more about why you should practise optimism.

The Greatness Guide, Robin Sharma (Harper Element, 2006)

The author of *The Monk Who Sold His Ferrari* writes a series of short chapters considering lessons he has learned during his career as a motivational guru. He also explains that guru literally means giver of light, which is a job title he feels comfortable with (and further justifies my own suggestions about challenging your title!).

The Houdini Solution: Why Thinking Inside the Box Is the Key to Creativity, Ernie Shenck (McGraw-Hill, 2006)

Using Harry Houdini as his inspiration, Shenck, an award-winning advertising executive, demonstrates how you can introduce creativity into your life.

Natural Born Winners, Robin Sieger (Arrow, 2004)
Robin Sieger is a man who recovered from cancer and found his life. He now works as a motivational speaker and in this book he shares his lessons for success.

How to Have an Outstanding Life, Paul Smith (New Holland, 2005)
A fantastically practical book by a famous Australian psychologist and sports fan, packed with great ideas about how to take control of your life and achieve the success you desire.

The Beermat Entrepreneur: Turn Your Good Idea into a Great Business, Mike Southon and Chris West (Prentice Hall, 2005)
This is a brilliant book for anyone who wants to start their own business or wants to begin a revolution in their workplace. It covers everything from the idea stage (in the pub) through to the day when you sell up to enjoy your millions.

All Too Human: A Political Education, George Stephanopoulos (Little, Brown, 2000)
An insight into the human side of the leadership of Bill Clinton when he was US President, as witnessed and recalled by one of his trusted advisers. It is also a fascinating insight into the political world behind the scenes.

Ahead of the Class, Marie Stubbs (John Murray, 2003)

An amazing story about retired headmistress Stubbs taking over a failing inner-city school and changing attitudes and results.

Mavericks at Work: Why the Most Original Minds in Business Win, **William Taylor and Polly LaBarre (Harper, 2008)**

The book on creativity in a working environment. If you want examples about how creativity can make winning teams, read about the computer programmers who compete like fighters, Cirque de Soleil's recruitment methods and HBO's unusual approach to TV programme making.

Break Out of the Box, **Mike Vance and Diane Deacon (Career Press, 1998)**

Mike Vance was Walt Disney's right-hand man in the 1960s and he introduces some of Disney's approach to creative thinking.

The Italian Job, **Gianluca Vialli and Gabrielle Marcotti (Bantam Books, 2007)**

Former football star Vialli writes this fascinating comparison between English and Italian football. He focuses on the role of leader in the two cultures and the whole book is an absorbing read.

Global Challenge: Leadership Lessons from the World's Toughest Yacht Race, **Humphrey Walters, Peter Mackie, Rose Mackie and Andrea Bacon (Book Guild, 1997)**

Humphrey Walters is the inspirational figure who supported Sir Clive Woodward's bold thinking to help England's rugby team to success. Before that, however, he joined the crew of the *BT Global Challenge* that raced around the world. He distils the lessons of leadership he learned on his travels in this fascinating book.

Winning: The Ultimate Business How-To Book, Jack Welch and Suzy Welch (HarperCollins, 2006)

The former head of GE's reflections on what makes a great leader, told in his own direct and accessible style.

Jack: Straight from the Gut, Jack Welch (Headline, 2003)

Welch's candid and frank autobiography, which details how he emerged from humble beginnings to become of the twentiety-century's most admired and respected business leaders.

The Luck Factor: The Scientific Study of the Lucky Mind, Richard Wiseman (Arrow, 2004)

A fascinating study of luck and how we can all learn to be lucky. It doesn't guarantee a Lottery win, but it does help you to appreciate what you do have.

Did You Spot the Gorilla? How to Recognize Hidden Opportunities, Richard Wiseman (Arrow, 2004)

Another interesting book by Richard Wiseman, which looks at how to spot the great opportunities that exist in our everyday lives.

Smart Leadership, Jonathan Yudelowitz, Richard Koch and Robin Field (Capstone, 2004)

Some useful leadership tips in an easily accessible book.